EACH · SINGING · WHAT · BELONGS · TO
HIM · OR · HER · AND · TO · NONE · ELSE

THE
POET'S CRAFT

Verses selected by
Helen Fern Daringer
&
Anne Thaxter Eaton

Illustrated by
Helene Carter

Granger Index Reprint Series

BOOKS FOR LIBRARIES PRESS
Freeport, New York

Library of Congress Cataloging in Publication Data

Daringer, Helen Fern, 1892-   comp.
   The poet's craft.

   (Granger index reprint series)
   1. English poetry (Collections) 2. American
poetry (Collections) I. Eaton, Annie Thaxter, joint
comp. II. Title.
PRII75.D27 1972   821'.008   72-8284
ISBN 0-8369-6385-7

PRINTED IN THE UNITED STATES OF AMERICA

CONTENTS

[v]

[vi]

[x]

ACKNOWLEDGMENTS

The authors of *The Poet's Craft* are grateful to the following poets and publishers for their kind permission to reprint selections for which they hold copyright.

James Branch Cabell for "Story of the Flowery Kingdom."

Ethel Kelley for "I've Got a Dog!"

George Allen and Unwin for Gilbert Murray's lines, "Longing," from his translation of Euripides.

D. Appleton-Century Company for Tudor Jenks's "Small and Early" from *St. Nicholas Magazine;* copyright 1889 by The Century Company.

The Bobbs-Merrill Company for "The Beetle" from *Rhymes of Childhood* by James Whitcomb Riley; copyright 1898 and 1918. Used by special permission of the publishers.

Child Life and Beatrice Curtis Brown for "Jonathan Bing"; *Child Life* and Mrs. Mildred Plew Merryman for "Pirate Don Durk of Dowdee."

Coward-McCann for "The Mouse" and "To a Black Dog, Bereaved," from *Compass Rose* by Elizabeth Coatsworth; copyright 1929 by Coward-McCann, Inc.

Thomas Y. Crowell and Charles K. Bolton for Sarah Knowles Bolton's "The Inevitable" from *The Inevitable and Other Poems.*

Doubleday, Doran and Company for "Forgiveness Lane" from *Within the Hedge* by Martha Gilbert Dickinson, copyright 1899 by Doubleday, Doran and Company, Inc.; and "Animal Crackers" from *Chimney Smoke* by Christopher Morley, copyright 1921 by Doubleday, Doran and Company, Inc.

E. P. Dutton and Company for Katharine Lee Bates's "Vigi" from *Sigurd, Our Golden Collie.*

Harper and Brothers and Arthur Guiterman for "Little Lost Pup" from *The Laughing Muse* by Arthur Guiterman.

Henry Holt and Company for Walter de la Mare's "The Listeners" and "Silver" from his *Collected Poems;* Robert Frost's "Stopping by Woods on a Snowy Evening" from *New Hampshire Poems;* Carl Sandburg's "At a Window" and "Theme in Yellow" from *Chicago Poems;* and Lew Sarett's "Four Little Foxes" from *Slow Smoke.*

Houghton Mifflin Company for Charles E. Carryl's "Robinson Crusoe's Story" from *Davy and the Goblin* and "The Post Captain" from *The Admiral's Caravan;* John Hay's "Jim Bludso" from his *Collected Poems;* H. H. Knibbs's "The Valley That God Forgot" from *Songs of the*

Trail; Edward Rowland Sills's "Opportunity" from his *Collected Poems;* Bayard Taylor's "A Story for a Child" from his *Collected Poems;* and James T. Trowbridge's "Vagabonds" from his *Poetical Works.* The poems by Emerson, Holmes, Longfellow, Lowell, and Whittier are used by permission of, and by special arrangement with, Houghton Mifflin Company, the authorized publishers.

Little, Brown and Company and Nancy Byrd Turner for "Boy, Bare Your Head" and "Courage Has a Crimson Coat" by Miss Turner, from *The Atlantic Readers, Book One,* edited by R. J. Condon. Also Emily Dickinson's "The Railway Train" from *The Poems of Emily Dickinson,* Centenary Edition, edited by Martha Dickinson Bianchi and Alfred Leete Hampson; and "A Last Prayer" from *Sonnets and Lyrics* by Helen Hunt Jackson. All reprinted by permission of Little, Brown and Company.

Longmans, Green and Company for Andrew Lang's "Romance" and "Scythe Song" from his *Poetical Works.*

The Macmillan Company for Ralph Hodgson's "Time, You Old Gipsy Man" from his *Poems;* and John Masefield's "Sea Fever" and "Spanish Waters" from his *Collected Poems.*

Punch for A. P. Herbert's "The Chameleon," and for "When You Go to Fairyland," which are reprinted by permission of the Proprietors of *Punch.*

G. P. Putnam's Sons for Charles Stuart Calverley's "Ballad," "Play," and "Shelter" from *Verses and Fly Leaves;* also to the publisher and to Dr. Thomas McCrae for "In Flanders Field" by John McCrae.

Charles Scribner's Sons for Eugene Field's "Little Boy Blue" from *With Trumpet and Drums;* George Meredith's "Song in the Songless" from his *Collected Poems;* Edwin Arlington Robinson's "The House on the Hill," from *The Children of the Night;* Henry van Dyke's "America for Me" and "Four Things" from his *Collected Poems;* and Sidney Lanier's "Song of the Chattahoochee" from *Poems of Sidney Lanier.*

The Southwest Press for Grace Noll Crowell's "Recompense" from *White Fire;* also to the Southwest Press and Karle Wilson Baker for Mrs. Baker's "City Lights," "A Child's Game," and "Morning Song" from *Dreamers on Horseback.*

Frederick A. Stokes Company for Alfred Noyes's "The Highwayman" and "A Song of Sherwood" from his *Collected Poems, Volume One;* copyright, 1906, by Frederick A. Stokes Company.

The Viking Press for "Clay Hills" from *Growing Pains* by Jean Starr Untermeyer; copyright, 1918, by B. W. Huebsch. Published by The Viking Press, Inc., New York.

To the Reader:

What matters about poetry is not that you should learn definitions of it, but that it should give you pleasure.

Begin where you choose and read wherever it pleases you. Some verse you will like at first sight; with other verse acquaintance will ripen more slowly; and it may be that for some you will never care. For poems, as you may already have discovered, resemble people, some lending themselves at once to friendship while others require longer acquaintance.

Poetry is an art. All the arts — poetry, music, painting, and the rest — yield most to the person who understands something of the practice of the art. How much enjoyment do you think a visitor from Mars would find in watching an American baseball game? Knowing nothing about the rules of the game or its purpose, he would be puzzled indeed to see such strange, apparently aimless antics as the players perform. He would be unable to share the enthusiasm that prompted other spectators to leap shouting from their seats. It is as true for the art of poetry as for the game of baseball that an understanding of "the rules of the game" increases one's enjoyment.

All poetry is meant to be read aloud. Your own voice saying the words and your own ears listening to the music of the lines make you feel the charm of verse, though you may not be able to describe it in words. If you know something about how poems are made, how the maker of verse weaves words into patterns of beauty, you will take even keener delight in reading poetry.

The poet's craft is as old as civilization. His materials are as familiar as daily bread — thoughts and moods, words and music. Once you have been initiated into the craft of poetry, you discover that your eyes are opened to new beauty in the world of everyday things about you, and that your ears are quickened to music of which you have been hitherto unaware.

A great poet once said that poetry makes immortal all that is best and most beautiful in the world. Certainly it is true that poetry preserves thoughts that would otherwise have vanished away; it keeps men and women, boys and girls, that would otherwise long since have been forgotten; dogs faithful to their masters, and kittens tumbling in the sun; deeds that were kind and courageous, and merry, lovable laughter.

This is your heritage — the accumulated treasure of centuries. Enter into possession of it.

Helen Fern Daringer
Anne Thaxter Eaton

I: RHYTHM

Shadows creep from the corners. The bird in the cage has stopped his singing. You are alone in the house. You listen. . . . The shadows deepen, the clock on the wall ticks hollowly. . . .

The sound of footsteps echoes through the dusk. But even while you are holding your breath to hear them, the approaching sounds resolve themselves into a familiar pattern. Rat *tat*, rat *tat*, rat *tat!* It is Father. You would recognize his step anywhere — a light step, a heavy step, a light step, a heavy step — brisk, firm, and vigorous, the right foot always coming down with a little heavier accent than the left.

The step of anybody else in the family you would recognize as easily. Light and quick for Mother — *tip* tap, *tip* tap, the first step more sharply accented than the second. Deliberate and slow for Grandfather, with his cane tapping two light strokes for each heavy footfall — tip tip *tlop*, tip tip *tlop*, tip tip *tlop*.

Each person's step makes its own pattern of sound. With a little practice, you could imitate different footsteps on the drum — the loud pounding steps of a boy running over the pavement, the halting shuffle of a blind man, the quick *left right, left right, left right* of a troop of marching soldiers. This regular recurrence of light and heavy accents is called rhythm.

Many movements have rhythm. The skillful rower lifts and lowers his oars with rhythmic regularity. The person who does not know how to row, like the person who is just learning to swim, is awkward and jerky. The expert skater glides over the ice with strokes of measured precision; the poor skater wobbles uncertainly. Breathing has rhythm, quiet and slow in sleep, fast and labored in running.

Year after year, the seasons return with rhythmic regularity — spring, summer, autumn, winter. The alternation of day and night, the rise and fall of ocean's tides, the waxing and waning of the moon in the starry heavens — these are rhythmic motions as truly as the pulse which beats in your own wrist.

Rhythm, then, is not something new and artificial. It is not something which musicians and poets have invented. It is as old as the tides in the sea, and as natural as breathing.

Read aloud for your own pleasure the poems that follow. In one you may hear the echo of galloping hoof-beats; in another, the slow tolling of a funeral knell. Some of the rhythms dance a jig, like Sir Peter Bombazoo. Some march like soldiers, and some are quiet as a lullaby. The rhythm of one of the poems is so irregular that it sounds more like ordinary speech than the measured movement of poetry.

The Post Captain

CHARLES EDWARD CARRYL

*A jolly, jigging rhythm is this.   It dances as lightly as Sir Peter's fingers
up and down the buttons of his coat.*

Post captain at the Needles and commander of a crew
On the Royal Biddy frigate was Sir Peter Bombazoo;
His mind was full of music and his head was full of tunes,
And he cheerfully exhibited on pleasant afternoons.

He could whistle, on his fingers, an invigorating reel,
And could imitate a piper on the handles of the wheel;
He could play in double octaves too, all up and down the
        rail,
Or rattle off a rondo on the bottom of a pail.

Then porters with their packages and bakers with their
        buns,
And countesses in carriages and grenadiers with guns,
And admirals and commodores arrived from near and far,
To listen to the music of this entertaining tar.

When they heard the Captain humming and beheld the
        dancing crew,
The commodores severely said, "Why, this will never do!"
And the admirals all hurried home, remarking, "This is
        most
Extraordinary conduct for a captain at his post."

Then they sent some sailing orders to Sir Peter, in a boat,
And he did a little fifing on the edges of the note;
But he read the sailing orders, as of course he had to do,
And removed the Royal Biddy to the Bay of Boohgabooh.

Now, Sir Peter took it kindly, but it's proper to explain,
He was sent to catch a pirate out upon the Spanish Main;
And he played, with variations, an imaginary tune
On the buttons of his waistcoat, like a jocular bassoon.

Then a topman saw the Pirate come a-sailing in the bay,
And reported to the Captain in the customary way.
"I'll receive him," said Sir Peter, "with a musical salute!"
And he gave some imitations of a double-jointed flute.

Then the Pirate cried derisively, "I've heard it done before!"
And he hoisted up a banner emblematical of gore.
But Sir Peter said serenely, "You may double-shot the guns
While I sing my little ballad of 'The Butter on the Buns.' "

Then the Pirate banged Sir Peter and Sir Peter banged him
    back,
And they banged away together as they took another tack.
Then Sir Peter said politely, "You may board him if you
    like " —
And he played a little dirge upon the handle of a pike.

Then the "Biddies" poured like hornets down upon the
    Pirate's deck,
And Sir Peter caught the Pirate and he took him by the
    neck,
And remarked, "You must excuse me, but you acted like a
    brute
When I gave my imitation of that double-jointed flute."
[6]

So they took that wicked Pirate and they took his wicked
        crew,
And tied them up in double knots in packages of two,
And left them lying on their backs in rows upon the beach
With a little bread and water within comfortable reach.

Now the Pirate had a treasure (mostly silverware and gold),
And Sir Peter took and stowed it in the bottom of his hold;
And said, "I will retire on this cargo of doubloons,
And each of you, my gallant crew, may have some silver
        spoons."

Now commodores in coach-and-fours and corporals in cabs,
And men with carts of pies and tarts and fishermen with
        crabs,
And barristers with wigs, in gigs, still gather on the strand —
But there isn't any music save a little German band.

Spanish Waters

John Masefield

The musical recurrent wash of the waters almost compels you to believe in the old sailor's tale of buried treasure.

Spanish waters, Spanish waters, you are ringing in my
    ears,
Like a slow sweet piece of music from the gray forgotten
    'years;
Telling tales, and beating tunes, and bringing weary
    thoughts to me
Of the sandy beach at Muertos, where I would that I
    could be.

There's a surf breaks on Los Muertos, and it never stops to
    roar,
And it's there we came to anchor, and it's there we went
    ashore,
Where the blue lagoon is silent amid snags of rotting trees,
Dropping like the clothes of corpses cast up by the seas.

We anchored at Los Muertos when the dipping sun was
    red,
We left her half a mile to sea, to west of Nigger Head;
And before the mist was on the Cay, before the day was
    done,
We were all ashore on Muertos with the gold that we had
    won.

We bore it through the marshes in a half-score battered
　　chests,
Sinking, in the sucking quagmires, to the sunburn on our
　　breasts,
Heaving over tree trunks, gasping, damning at the flies and
　　heat,
Longing for a long drink, out of silver, in the ship's cool
　　lazareet.

The moon came white and ghostly as we laid the treasure
　　down,
There was gear there'd make a beggarman as rich as Lima
　　Town,
Copper charms and silver trinkets from the chests of Span-
　　ish crews,
Gold doubloons and double moidores, louis d'ors and
　　portagues,

Clumsy yellow-metal earrings from the Indians of
　　Brazil,
Uncut emeralds out of Rio, bezoar stones from Guayaquil;
Silver, in the crude and fashioned, pots of old Arica bronze,
Jewels from the bones of Incas desecrated by the Dons.

We smoothed the place with mattocks, and we took and
　　blazed the tree,
Which marks yon where the gear is hid that none will ever
　　see,
And we laid aboard the ship again, and south away we
　　steers,
Through the loud surf of Los Muertos which is beating in
　　my ears.

I'm the last alive that knows it.   All the rest have gone
      their ways,
Killed, or died, or come to anchor in the old Mulatas Cays,
And I go singing, fiddling, old and starved and in despair,
And I know where all that gold is hid, if I were only there.

It's not the way to end it all.   I'm old, and nearly blind,
And an old man's past's a strange thing, for it never leaves
      his mind.
And I see in dreams, awhiles, the beach, the sun's disc dip-
      ping red,
And the tall ship, under topsails, swaying in past Nigger
      Head.

I'd be glad to step ashore there.   Glad to take a pick and
      go
To the lone blazed coco-palm tree in the place no others
      know,
And lift the gold and silver that has mouldered there for
      years
By the loud surf of Los Muertos which is beating in my ears.

Pirate Don Durk of Dowdee

MILDRED PLEW MERRYMAN

*Nobody but a pirate could walk through a poem with such a light-hearted,
swashbuckling rhythm.*

Ho, for the Pirate Don Durk of Dowdee!
He was as wicked as wicked could be,
But oh, he was perfectly gorgeous to see!
     The Pirate Don Durk of Dowdee.

His conscience, of course, was as black as a bat,
But he had a floppety plume on his hat
And when he went walking it jiggled — like that!
     The plume of the Pirate Dowdee.

His coat it was crimson and cut with a slash,
And often as ever he twirled his mustache
Deep down in the ocean the mermaids went splash,
     Because of Don Durk of Dowdee.

Moreover, Dowdee had a purple tattoo,
And stuck in his belt where he buckled it through
Were a dagger, a dirk, and a squizzamaroo,
     For fierce was the Pirate Dowdee.

So fearful he was, he would shoot at a puff,
And always at sea when the weather grew rough
He drank from a bottle and wrote on his cuff,
     Did Pirate Don Durk of Dowdee.

Oh, he had a cutlass that swung at his thigh
And he had a parrot called Pepperkin Pye,
And a zigzaggy scar at the end of his eye
    Had Pirate Don Durk of Dowdee.

He kept in a cavern, this buccaneer bold,
A curious chest that was covered with mould,
And all of his pockets were jingly with gold!
    Oh jing! went the gold of Dowdee.

His conscience, of course, it was crook'd like a squash,
But both of his boots made a slickery slosh,
And he went through the world with a wonderful swash,
    Did Pirate Don Durk of Dowdee.

It's true he was wicked as wicked could be,
His sins they outnumbered a hundred and three,
But oh, he was perfectly gorgeous to see!
    The Pirate Don Durk of Dowdee.

Story of the Flowery Kingdom

JAMES BRANCH CABELL

A gay, smooth rhythm has this verse — perhaps because the Dragon smoothed out the rough spots.

Fair Sou-Chong-Tee, by a shimmering brook
Where ghost-like lilies loomed tall and straight,
Met young Too-Hi, in a moonlit nook,
Where they cooed and kissed till the hour was late:
Then, with lanterns, a mandarin passed in state,
Named Hoo-Hung-Hoo of the Golden Band,
Who had wooed the maiden to be *his* mate —
For these things occur in the Flowery Land.

Now, Hoo-Hung-Hoo had written a book,
In seven volumes, to celebrate
The death of the Emperor's thirteenth cook:
So, being a person whose power was great,
He ordered a herald to indicate
He would blind Too-Hi with a red-hot brand
And marry Sou-Chong at a quarter-past eight —
For these things occur in the Flowery Land.

Whilst the brand was heating, the lovers shook
In their several shoes, — when by lucky fate
A Dragon came, with his tail in a crook —
A Dragon out of a Nankeen Plate —
And gobbled the hard-hearted potentate
And all of his servants, and snorted, *and*
Passed on at a super-cyclonic rate —
For these things occur in the Flowery Land.

[13]

The lovers were wed at an early date,
And lived for the future, I understand,
In one continuous tête-à-tête —
For these things occur . . . in the Flowery Land.

Horses of the Sea

CHRISTINA ROSSETTI

◄··

The horses of the sea and of the field do not clatter and gallop.
They move quietly and stay close at home.

◄··

T he horses of the sea
Rear a foaming crest,
But the horses of the land
Serve us the best.

The horses of the land
Munch corn and clover,
While the foaming sea-horses
Toss and turn over.

Lochinvar

Sir Walter Scott

*Young Lochinvar does not ride a gentle ambling steed when he goes to
rescue fair Ellen. The lines echo the hoof-beats of a galloping war horse.*

O young Lochinvar is come out of the west,
Through all the wide Border his steed was the best;
And, save his good broadsword, he weapon had none,
He rode all unarmed, and he rode all alone.
So faithful in love, and so dauntless in war,
There never was knight like the young Lochinvar.

He stayed not for brake, and he stopped not for stone,
He swam the Eske River where ford there was none;
But ere he alighted at Netherby gate,
The bride had consented, the gallant came late:
For a laggard in love, and a dastard in war,
Was to wed the fair Ellen of brave Lochinvar.

So boldly he entered the Netherby Hall,
Among bridesmen and kinsmen and brothers and all:
Then spoke the bride's father, his hand on his sword,
(For the poor craven bridegroom said never a word),
"O, come ye in peace here, or come ye in war,
Or to dance at our bridal, young Lord Lochinvar?"

"I long wooed your daughter, my suit you denied; —
Love swells like the Solway, but ebbs like its tide, —
And now am I come, with this lost love of mine,
To lead but one measure, drink one cup of wine.
There are maidens in Scotland more lovely by far,
That would gladly be bride to the young Lochinvar."

[15]

The bride kissed the goblet; the knight took it up,
He quaffed off the wine, and he threw down the cup.
She looked down to blush, and she looked up to sigh,
With a smile on her lips and a tear in her eye.
He took her soft hand ere her mother could bar, —
"Now tread we a measure!" said young Lochinvar.

So stately his form, and so lovely her face,
That never a hall such a galliard did grace;
While her mother did fret, and her father did fume,
And the bridegroom stood dangling his bonnet and plume;
And the bride-maidens whispered, "'Twere better by far,
To have matched our fair cousin with young Lochinvar."

One touch to her hand, and one word in her ear,
When they reached the hall door, and the charger stood near;
So light to the croupe the fair lady he swung,
So light to the saddle before her he sprung!
"She is won! we are gone, over bank, bush, and scaur!
They'll have fleet steeds that follow," quoth young Lochinvar.

There was mounting 'mong Graemes of the Netherby clan;
Forsters, Fenwicks, and Musgraves, they rode and they ran:
There was racing and chasing on Cannobie Lee,
But the lost bride of Netherby ne'er did they see.
So daring in love, and so dauntless in war,
Have ye e'er heard of gallant like young Lochinvar?

A Song of Sherwood

ALFRED NOYES

As fleet as shadows and as noiseless as leaves in the greenwood, Robin Hood's band rides through the woods again.   Smoothly they swing in their saddles — these joyous ghosts of long ago.

Sherwood in the twilight, is Robin Hood awake?
Gray and ghostly shadows are gliding through the brake,
Shadows of the dappled deer, dreaming of the morn,
Dreaming of a shadowy man that winds a shadowy horn.

Robin Hood is here again: all his merry thieves
Hear a ghostly bugle note shivering through the leaves,
Calling as he used to call, faint and far away,
In Sherwood, in Sherwood, about the break of day.

Merry, merry England has kissed the lips of June:
All the wings of fairyland were here beneath the moon,
Like a flight of rose leaves fluttering in a mist
Of opal and ruby and pearl and amethyst.

Merry, merry England is waking as of old,
With eyes of blither hazel and hair of brighter gold:
For Robin Hood is here again beneath the bursting spray
In Sherwood, in Sherwood, about the break of day.

Love is in the greenwood building him a house
Of wild rose and hawthorn and honeysuckle boughs:
Love is in the greenwood; dawn is in the skies;
And Marian is waiting with a glory in her eyes.

Hark! The dazzled laverock climbs the golden steep!
Marian is waiting: is Robin Hood asleep?
Round the fairy grass-rings frolic elf and fay,
In Sherwood, in Sherwood, about the break of day.

Oberon, Oberon, rake away the gold,
Rake away the red leaves, roll away the mould,
Rake away the gold leaves, roll away the red,
And wake Will Scarlett from his leafy forest bed.

Friar Tuck and Little John are riding down together
With quarterstaff and drinking can and gray goose feather.
The dead are coming back again, the years are rolled away
In Sherwood, in Sherwood, about the break of day.

Softly over Sherwood the south wind blows;
All the heart of England hid in every rose
Hears across the greenwood the sunny whisper leap,
Sherwood in the red dawn, is Robin Hood asleep?

Hark, the voice of England wakes him as of old
And, shattering the silence with a cry of brighter gold,
Bugles in the greenwood echo from the steep,
Sherwood in the red dawn, is Robin Hood asleep?

Where the deer are gliding down the shadowy glen
All across the glades of fern he calls his merry men —
Doublets of the Lincoln green glancing through the May
In Sherwood, in Sherwood, about the break of day —

Calls them and they answer: from aisles of oak and ash
Rings the *Follow! Follow!* and the boughs begin to crash,
The ferns begin to flutter and the flowers begin to fly,
And through the crimson dawning the robber band goes by.
[18]

Robin! Robin! Robin! All his merry thieves
Answer as the bugle note shivers through the leaves,
Calling as he used to call, faint and far away,
In Sherwood, in Sherwood, about the break of day.

Hawthorn shrubs, called the *May*, with their white and pink blossoms,
are common in the English countryside. The *laverock* is the lark, soaring
toward the golden dawn.

Robin Hood

JOHN KEATS

The rhythm is as light as a breeze in the forest.

On the fairest time of June
You may go, with sun or moon,
Or the seven stars to light you,
Or the polar ray to right you,
But you never may behold
Little John or Robin bold;
Never one, of all the clan,
Thrumming on an empty can
Some old hunting ditty, while
He doth his green way beguile
To fair hostess Merriment
Down beside the pasture Trent.

The Charge of the Light Brigade

ALFRED, LORD TENNYSON

This poem takes its rhythm from the thunder of cannon and the gallop of charging horses. Notice how the repetition of lines suggests the repeated assaults of the soldiers and the continued thundering of the cannon.

Half a league, half a league,
Half a league onward,
All in the valley of Death
   Rode the six hundred.
"Forward, the Light Brigade!
Charge for the guns!" he said:
Into the valley of Death
   Rode the six hundred.

"Forward, the Light Brigade!"
Was there a man dismayed?
Not though the soldier knew
   Someone had blundered:
Theirs not to make reply,
Theirs not to reason why,
Theirs but to do and die:
Into the valley of Death
   Rode the six hundred.

Cannon to right of them,
Cannon to left of them,
Cannon in front of them
   Volleyed and thundered;
Stormed at with shot and shell,
Boldly they rode and well,

Into the jaws of Death,
Into the mouth of Hell
Rode the six hundred.

Flashed all their sabers bare,
Flashed as they turned in air
Sabring the gunners there,
Charging an army, while
All the world wondered:
Plunged in the battery smoke
Right through the line they broke;
Cossack and Russian
Reeled from the saber stroke,
Shattered and sundered.
Then they rode back, but not —
Not the six hundred.

Cannon to right of them,
Cannon to left of them,
Cannon behind them
Volleyed and thundered;
Stormed at with shot and shell,
While horse and hero fell,
They that had fought so well
Came through the jaws of Death,
Back from the mouth of Hell,
All that was left of them,
Left of six hundred.

When can their glory fade?
O the wild charge they made!
All the world wondered.
Honor the charge they made!
Honor the Light Brigade,
Noble six hundred!

Ode on
the Duke of Wellington

ALFRED, LORD TENNYSON

While the long procession follows to his grave the hero who conquered Napoleon, the air reverberates with the heavy tolling of his funeral knell. These stanzas are part of a long poem.

Bury the Great Duke
   With an empire's lamentation,
Let us bury the Great Duke
   To the noise of the mourning of a mighty nation,
Mourning when their leaders fall:
Warriors carry the warrior's pall,
And sorrow darkens hamlet and hall.

Where shall we lay the man whom we deplore?
Here, in streaming London's central roar.
Let the sound of those he wrought for,
And the feet of those he fought for,
Echo round his bones for evermore.

Lead out the pageant: sad and slow,
As fits an universal woe,
Let the long, long procession go,
And let the sorrowing crowd about it grow,
And let the mournful martial music blow;
The last great Englishman is low.

All is over and done:
Render thanks to the Giver,
England, for thy son.
Let the bell be tolled.
Render thanks to the Giver,
And render him to the mould.
Under the cross of gold
That shines over city and river,
There he shall rest forever
Among the wise and bold.
Let the bell be tolled
And a reverent people behold
The towering car, the sable steeds:
Bright let it be with its blazoned deeds,
Dark in its funeral fold.
Let the bell be tolled:
And a deeper knell in the heart be knolled.

A Child's Game

KARLE WILSON BAKER

The ordered, quiet rhythm to which these lines move seems just suited to express a child's thought of death.

Nor sleep, nor journey, nor affray
Can justly image death to me:
I am a little child, and Death
The one who lets you go and see.

All children in a darkened room;
And Death stands smiling at the door,
His finger on his lips, and says
So quietly, "Now, one child more!"

I have so longed and longed to know
What lovely things the children find
When they have gone beyond the door;
But not a child that's left behind

Has ever been; for when they go
He will not ever let them back:
And when he beckons them, and we
Stand tiptoe, watching for the crack,

Our strange sweet playmate steps between
And will not let us see at all;
He smiles at our expectancy
With "You may come too, when I call."

And oh, within the darkened room,
I have so longed and longed to know
Just what it is they see and learn,
The other children, when they go.

Do you suppose that I shall feel
Afraid, to see him look at me,
At last, and beckon with his hand,
And smile, "Now *you* may go and see"?

Curfew

HENRY WADSWORTH LONGFELLOW

*A single bell is ringing in the darkness, with slow and measured
stroke.*

Solemnly, mournfully,
    Dealing its dole,
The Curfew Bell
    Is beginning to toll.

Cover the embers,
    And put out the light;
Toil comes with the morning,
    And rest with the night.

Dark grow the windows,
    And quenched is the fire;
Sound fades into silence, —
    All footsteps retire.

No voice in the chambers,
    No sound in the hall!
Sleep and oblivion
    Reign over all!

The book is completed,
    And closed, like the day;
And the hand that has written it
    Lays it away.

Dim grow its fancies;
    Forgotten they lie;
Like coals in the ashes,
    They darken and die.

Song sinks into silence,
    The story is told,
The windows are darkened,
    The hearthstone is cold.

Darker and darker
    The black shadows fall;
Sleep and oblivion
    Reign over all.

The Merman

ALFRED, LORD TENNYSON

The words of the poem are as persuasive as a soft sea breeze.

Who would be
A merman bold,
Sitting alone,
Singing alone
Under the sea,
With a crown of gold,
On a throne?

I would be a merman bold;
I would sit and sing the whole of the day;
I would fill the sea-halls with a voice of power
But at night I would roam abroad and play
With the mermaids in and out of the rocks,
Dressing their hair with the white sea-flower;
And holding them back by their flowing locks
I would kiss them often under the sea,
And kiss them again, till they kissed me
    Laughingly, laughingly;
And then we would wander away, away,
To the pale sea-groves straight and high
    Chasing each other merrily.

The Indian Woman

WALT WHITMAN

All speech has some rhythm. The rhythm of everyday speech, however, is not smooth and regular. It resembles the broken rhythms of Whitman's poem. These lines are from a longer poem, " The Sleeper."

Now I tell what my mother told me today as we sat at
    dinner together,
Of when she was a nearly grown girl, living home with her
    parents on the old homestead.
A red squaw came one breakfast-time to the old homestead,
On her back she carried a bundle of rushes for rush-bottom-
    ing chairs,
Her hair, straight, shiny, coarse, black, profuse, half-
    enveloped her face,
Her step was free and elastic, and her voice sounded
    exquisitely as she spoke.
My mother looked in delight and amazement at the
    stranger,
She looked at the freshness of her tall-borne face, and full
    and pliant limbs,
The more she looked upon her she loved her,
Never before had she seen such wonderful beauty and
    purity;
She made her sit on a bench by the jamb of the fireplace —
    she cooked food for her,
She had no work to give her, but she gave her remembrance
    and fondness.
The red squaw stayed all the forenoon, and toward the
    middle of the afternoon she went away,

O my mother was loath to have her go away!
All the week she thought of her — she watched for her for
        many a month,
She remembered her many a winter and many a summer,
But the red squaw never came, nor was heard of there again.

Theme in Yellow

CARL SANDBURG

*As you say these lines, don't they sound a little humpy and
bumpy, like pumpkins?*

I spot the hills
With yellow balls in autumn
I light the prairie cornfields
Orange and tawny gold clusters
And I am called pumpkins.
On the last of October
When dusk is fallen
Children join hands
And circle round me
Singing ghost songs
And love to the harvest moon;
I am a jack-o'-lantern
With terrible teeth
And the children know
I am fooling.

Ariel's Song

WILLIAM SHAKESPEARE

If there were nothing else in the poem to tell you, you would know from the light swinging rhythm that this is a fairy's song. It is taken from the play, " The Tempest."

Where the bee sucks, there suck I;
In a cowslip's bell I lie;
There I couch when owls do cry.
On the bat's back I do fly
After summer merrily.
Merrily, merrily, shall I live now,
Under the blossom that hangs on the bough.

II: RHYTHM AND EMOTION

How solemn is the muffled slow beat of the soldier's funeral drum! How lively the same drum's quick-marching *rat*-a-tat-*tat*, *rat*-a-tat-*tat!*

The drumsticks beat a merry tattoo, and your heart quickens. Your feet would like to dance to the lilting rhythm. Life is good and you are free of care. You feel the gladness of the world when the drum sounds. . . . There comes a change in the pattern of the drumbeats. They strike in slow succession. They seem dull and weighted. They thud heavily. Your step grows heavy, and your heart too, answering the sad rhythm of the drum.

Primitive people knew the power of rhythm. Their tom-toms thundered courage before a battle, and afterward exulted in the victory won. Not satisfied merely to listen, the warriors danced to the music of the pounding drums and emphasized the rhythm by shouting or chanting in unison.

The poet understands the close kinship between rhythm and the emotions. He knows that rhythmic language best expresses his feelings. He knows too that rhythm not only gives pleasure to his readers, but helps them to understand and share his feeling.

"The song ends in silence. The story has been told. Windows are dark. The hearth is cold," says the writer of prose. His words have the same meaning as the poet's, but they lack in rhythm. Lacking that, they are neither so beautiful nor so charged with emotion as these lines.

> Song sinks into silence,
> The story is told,
> The windows are darkened,
> The hearthstone is cold.

[31]

A foreigner, even though he did not understand the meaning of the words, could tell by the swing of the lines which of these stanzas belongs to a rollicking poem and which to a serious one.

> When mortals are at rest,
> And snoring in their nest,
> Unheard, and unespied,
> Through keyholes we do glide;
> Over tables, stools, and shelves,
> We trip it with our Fairy Elves.

> Lead out the pageant: sad and slow,
> As fits an universal woe,
> Let the long, long procession go,
> And let the sorrowing crowd about it grow,
> And let the mournful martial music blow;
> The last great Englishman is low.

You will find your own moods reflected in the rhythmic words of the poets, as sunny skies and gray are mirrored in the clear waters of the mountain lake.

The Railway Train

EMILY DICKINSON

The rhythm of these lines is vigorous and strong, like the movement of a speeding locomotive.

I like to see it lap the miles,
And lick the valleys up,
And stop to feed itself at tanks;
And then, prodigious, step

Around a pile of mountains,
And, supercilious, peer
In shanties by the sides of roads;
And then a quarry pare

To fit its sides, and crawl between,
Complaining all the while
In horrid, hooting stanza;
Then chase itself down hill

And neigh like Boanerges;
Then, punctual as a star,
Stop — docile and omnipotent —
At its own stable door.

The old Biblical term *Boanerges* means sons of thunder.

Sea Fever

John Masefield

The long, rolling gait of the sailor carries you with him in spirit while you read — away from crowds and cities, down to the sea and freedom.

I must go down to the seas again, to the lonely sea and the
    sky,
And all I ask is a tall ship and a star to steer her by;
And the wheel's kick and the wind's song and the white
    sail's shaking,
And a gray mist on the sea's face and a gray dawn breaking.

I must go down to the seas again, for the call of the running
    tide
Is a wild call and a clear call that may not be denied;
And all I ask is a windy day with white clouds flying,
And the flung spray and the blown spume, and the seagulls
    crying.

I must go down to the seas again, to the vagrant gypsy life,
To the gull's way and the whale's way where the wind's like
    a whetted knife;
And all I ask is a merry yarn from a laughing fellow-rover,
And quiet sleep and a sweet dream when the long trick's
    over.

Recompense

GRACE NOLL CROWELL

The quiet pictures and even flow of the poet's thoughts stamp the rhythm of her verse with quiet grace.

I never have had a look at the sea,
I who would love it so.
I never have watched from the surf-drenched shore
The brave ships come and go.
I do not know how the silent tides
Unfailingly ebb and flow.

God who is wise to His children's needs,
Gives me the wide low plain,
He gives me the wondrous, whispering grass,
The kildee's sweet refrain,
And my reed-fringed pools are myriad seas,
After the last long rain.

I never have been where the mountains stand
Majestic — aloof — apart —
But nightly the infinite star-crowned heights
Speak to my waiting heart,
And mine are the winds that are mountain-born,
And of seas they are a part.

I Hear America Singing

WALT WHITMAN

The poet hears America singing a vigorous chorus of many different tunes and rhythms.

I hear America singing, the varied carols I hear,
Those of mechanics, each one singing his as it should be,
    blithe and strong,
The carpenter singing his as he measures his plank or beam,
The mason singing his as he makes ready for work, or leaves
    off work,
The boatman singing what belongs to him in his boat, the
    deckhand singing on the steamboat deck,
The shoemaker singing as he sits on his bench, the hatter
    singing as he stands,
The woodcutter's song, the plowboy's on his way in the
    morning, or at noon intermission or at sundown,
The delicious singing of the mother, or of the young wife at
    work, or of the girl sewing or washing —
Each singing what belongs to him or her, and to none else,
The day what belongs to the day — at night the party of
    young fellows, robust, friendly,
Singing with open mouths their strong melodious songs.

The Flag Goes By

HENRY HOLCOMB BENNETT

It would be a very dull person, indeed, whose pulses were not quickened by such rousing measures as these.

Hats off!
Along the street there comes
A blare of bugles, a ruffle of drums,
A flash of color beneath the sky:
Hats off!
The flag is passing by!

Blue and crimson and white it shines,
Over the steel-tipped, ordered lines.
Hats off!
The colors before us fly;
But more than the flag is passing by.

Sea-fights and land-fights, grim and great,
Fought to make and to save the State:
Weary marches and sinking ships;
Cheers of victory on dying lips;

Days of plenty and years of peace;
March of a strong land's swift increase;
Equal justice, right and law,
Stately honor and reverend awe;

Sign of a nation, great and strong
To ward her people from foreign wrong:
Pride and glory and honor, — all
Live in the colors to stand or fall.

Hats off!
Along the street there comes
A blare of bugles, a ruffle of drums;
And loyal hearts are beating high:
Hats off!
The flag is passing by!

On a Quiet Conscience

CHARLES THE FIRST

These verses fall as quietly as sleep upon a quiet mind at a long day's end.

Close thine eyes, and sleep secure;
Thy soul is safe, thy body sure.
He that guards thee, He that keeps,
Never slumbers, never sleeps.
A quiet conscience in thy breast
Has only peace, has only rest.
The wisest and the mirth of kings
Are out of tune unless she sings:
Then close thine eyes in peace and sleep secure,
No sleep so sweet as thine, no rest so sure.

Oh, Dear!

The rhythm of this old song suggests two different emotions. Part of the time the maiden feels only how tiresome it is to wait for the laggard Johnny. Part of the time she is excited, thinking what gifts he will bring her. Do you notice any change in the movement of the stanzas to correspond to her changes of mood?

Oh, dear! what can the matter be?
Dear! dear! what can the matter be?
Oh, dear! what can the matter be?
Johnny's so long at the fair.

He promised he'd buy me a fairing should please me,
And then for a kiss, oh! he vowed he would tease me,
He promised he'd bring me a bunch of blue ribbons
To tie up my bonny brown hair.

And it's oh, dear! what can the matter be?
Dear! dear! what can the matter be?
Oh, dear! what can the matter be?
Johnny's so long at the fair.

He promised he'd bring me a basket of posies,
A garland of lilies, a garland of roses,
A little straw hat, to set off the blue ribbons
That tie up my bonny brown hair.

And it's oh, dear! what can the matter be?
Dear! dear! what can the matter be?
Oh, dear! what can the matter be?
Johnny's so long at the fair.

AN OLD SONG

Longing

GILBERT MURRAY

The speaker soars in imagination, swift as a bird and light as a cloud.
The rhythm of the lines is as effortless as the flight of wings.

Could I take me to some cavern for mine hiding,
In the hilltops where the Sun scarce hath trod;
Or a cloud to make the home of mine abiding,
As a bird among the bird droves of God!
Could I wing me to my rest amid the roar
Of the deep Adriatic on the shore,
Where the water of Eridanus is clear,
And Phaëthon's sad sisters by his grave
Weep into the river, and each tear
Gleams, a drop of amber, in the wave.

To the strand of the Daughters of the Sunset,
The Apple-tree, the singing and the gold;
Where the mariner must stay him from his onset,
And the red wave is tranquil as of old;
Yea, beyond that Pillar of the End
That Atlas guardeth, would I wend;
Where a voice of living waters never ceaseth
In God's quiet garden by the sea,
And Earth, the ancient life-giver, increaseth
Joy among the meadows like a tree.

The poet would fly far, to the river where Phaëthon's sisters weep for the lad who tried to drive the chariot of the Sun. Farther yet he longs to go, to the Island of the Sunset, where grow the golden apples guarded by fair nymphs; and farther still, beyond the pillars that hold earth and sky apart at the world's end. This poem was translated from a Greek play, *Hippolytus*, written by Euripides about 450 B.C.

City Lights

KARLE WILSON BAKER

This is almost a frolicsome rhythm, and the last stanza is even gayer than the first.

God made, they say, the country
And man, they say, the town —
But God forgets his handiwork
When the sun goes down!

Stars, to be sure, on lucky nights,
Moon, when her seasons fall —
The darlings won't work overtime:
They are too punctual.

Moon takes her rest on rainy nights
All muffled in her cloak;
She will not tramp the soggy lanes
With poor belated folk;

But ah, that is the very time
To see the pavement shine!
The gutter-child may then outstare
Aladdin in his mine.

God's a master-workman,
Man, a 'prentice-clown;
But God was in the heart of man
When he lit the town!

The Song of the Shirt

THOMAS HOOD

Because the poet wishes you to realize the wearisome monotony of the poor shirt-maker's life, he has her speak in a monotonous rhythm. Her voice seems to keep time with her tired needle's stitching.

With fingers weary and worn,
  With eyelids heavy and red,
A woman sat in unwomanly rags,
  Plying her needle and thread —
    Stitch! stitch! stitch!
In poverty, hunger, and dirt;
  And still with a voice of dolorous pitch
She sang the "Song of the Shirt!"

"Work! work! work!
  While the cock is crowing aloof!
And work — work — work
  Till the stars shine through the roof!
It's oh! to be a slave
  Along with the barbarous Turk,
Where woman has never a soul to save,
  If this is Christian work!

"Work — work — work
  Till the brain begins to swim;
Work — work — work
  Till the eyes are heavy and dim.
Seam, and gusset, and band,
  Band, and gusset, and seam —
Till over the buttons I fall asleep,
  And sew them on in a dream!

"Work — work — work!
    My labor never flags;
And what are its wages?   A bed of straw,
    A crust of bread — and rags.
That shattered roof — and this naked floor —
    A table — a broken chair —
And a wall so blank, my shadow I thank
    For sometimes falling there.

"Work — work — work,
    In the dull December light,
And work — work — work,
    When the weather is warm and bright;
While underneath the eaves
    The brooding swallows cling,
As if to show me their sunny backs
    And twit me with the spring.

"Oh, but to breathe the breath
    Of the cowslip and primrose sweet —
With the sky above my head,
    And the grass beneath my feet;
For only one short hour
    To feel as I used to feel,
Before I knew the woes of want
    And the walk that costs a meal.

"Oh, but for one short hour!
    A respite, however brief!
No blessed leisure for love or hope,
    But only time for grief!
A little weeping would ease my heart;
    But in their briny bed
My tears must stop, for every drop
    Hinders needle and thread!"

With fingers weary and worn,
　　With eyelids heavy and red,
A woman sat in unwomanly rags,
　　Plying her needle and thread —
　　　　Stitch! stitch! stitch!
In poverty, hunger, and dirt;
And still with a voice of dolorous pitch —
Would that its tone could reach the rich! —
She sang this "Song of the Shirt!"

Heraclitus

WILLIAM JOHNSON-CORY

The poet in thought addresses his lost friend, Heraclitus. Though the poet is sad, his words have not the slow, heavy movement of a dirge or funeral ode, because he remembers the happiness they had shared.

They told me, Heraclitus, they told me you were dead,
They brought me bitter news to hear and bitter tears to shed.
I wept as I remembered how often you and I
Had tired the sun with talking and sent him down the sky.

And now that thou art lying, my dear old Carian guest,
A handful of grey ashes, long, long ago at rest,
Still are thy pleasant voices, thy nightingales awake;
For death he taketh all away, but them he cannot take.

These lines were translated from an ancient Greek poem, written about 260 B.C. The guest came from *Caria*, a country in Asia Minor, near Greece.

The Shepherd's Psalm

What a comforting strength is in this poem! — not only in the meaning of the words but in the quiet steady march of the lines. It is the Twenty-third Psalm in the Bible.

The Lord is my shepherd; I shall not want.
He maketh me to lie down in green pastures;
He leadeth me beside the still waters.
He restoreth my soul:
He leadeth me in the paths of righteousness
For his name's sake.
Yea, though I walk through the valley of
    the shadow of death,
I will fear no evil: for thou art with me;
Thy rod and thy staff they comfort me.
Thou preparest a table before me
In the presence of mine enemies:
Thou anointest my head with oil;
My cup runneth over.
Surely goodness and mercy shall follow me
All the days of my life;
And I will dwell in the house of the Lord forever.

A Song of David

The Fairy Queen

*It is impossible to remain solemn while thinking of these
mischievous, nimble elves.*

Come, follow, follow me,
You Fairy Elves that be;
Which circle on the greene,
Come, follow Mab your Queene.
Hand in hand, let's dance around,
For this place is fairye ground.

When mortals are at rest,
And snoring in their nest,
Unheard, and unespied,
Through keyholes we do glide;
Over tables, stools, and shelves,
We trip it with our Fairy Elves.

And if the house be foul
With platter, dish, or bowl,
Upstairs we nimbly creep,
And find the sluts asleep:
There we pinch their armes and thighes:
None escapes, nor none espies.

But if the house be swept,
And from uncleanness kept,
We praise the household maid,
And duely she is paid:
For we use before we goe
To drop a tester in her shoe.

Upon a mushroome's head
Our tablecloth we spread;
A grain of rye or wheat
Is manchet, which we eat;
Pearly drops of dew we drink
In acorn cups filled to the brink.

The brains of nightingales,
With unctuous fat of snailes,
Between two cockles stewed,
Is meat that's easily chewed;
Tailes of wormes, and marrow of mice,
Do make a dish that's wonderous nice.

The grasshopper, gnat, and fly
Serve for our minstrelsie;
Grace said, we dance a while,
And so the time beguile:
And if the moon doth hide her head,
The gloe-worm lights us home to bed.

On tops of dewie grasse
So nimbly do we passe,
The young and tender stalk
Ne'er bends when we do walk:
Yet in the morning may be seen
Where we the night before have been.

AN OLD BALLAD

The *tester* dropped in a shoe is a coin, and the *manchet* is a loaf.

Robinson Crusoe's Story

CHARLES EDWARD CARRYL

Of course Robinson Crusoe says it was very sad and lonely, but do you think he means it? The rhythm certainly does not sound sad.

The night was thick and hazy
When the Piccadilly Daisy
Carried down the crew and captain in the sea;
   And I think the water drowned 'em;
   For they never, never found 'em,
And I know they didn't come ashore with me.

Oh! 'twas very sad and lonely
When I found myself the only
Population on this cultivated shore;
   But I've made a little tavern
   In a rocky little cavern,
And I sit and watch for people at the door.

I spent no time in looking
For a girl to do my cooking,
As I'm quite a clever hand at making stews;
   But I had that fellow Friday,
   Just to keep the tavern tidy,
And to put a Sunday polish on my shoes.

I have a little garden
That I'm cultivating lard in,
As the things I eat are rather tough and dry;
   For I live on toasted lizards,
   Prickly pears, and parrot gizzards,
And I'm really very fond of beetle pie.

The clothes I had were furry,
　And it made me fret and worry
When I found the moths were eating off the hair;
　And I had to scrape and sand 'em,
　And I boiled 'em and I tanned 'em,
Till I got the fine morocco suit I wear.

　I sometimes seek diversion
　In a family excursion
With the few domestic animals you see;
　And we take along a carrot
　As refreshment for the parrot,
And a little can of jungleberry tea.

　Then we gather, as we travel,
　Bits of moss and dirty gravel,
And we chip off little specimens of stone;
　And we carry home as prizes
　Funny bugs, of handy sizes,
Just to give the day a scientific tone.

　If the roads are wet and muddy,
　We remain at home and study, —
For the Goat is very clever at a sum, —
　And the Dog, instead of fighting,
　Studies ornamental writing,
While the Cat is taking lessons on the drum.

　We retire at eleven,
　And we rise again at seven;
And I wish to call attention, as I close,
　To the fact that all the scholars
　Are correct about their collars,
And particular in turning out their toes.

The Lobster Quadrille

Lewis Carroll

The snail and his friends are just about as sprightly in their dancing as they are in their thinking!

"Will you walk a little faster?" said a whiting to a snail;
"There's a porpoise close behind us, and he's treading on
my tail,
See how eagerly the lobsters and the turtles all advance!
They are waiting on the shingle — will you come and join
the dance?
Will you, won't you, will you, won't you, will you join
the dance?
Will you, won't you, will you, won't you, won't you join
the dance?

"You can really have no notion how delightful it will
be
When they take us up and throw us, with the lobsters, out to
sea!"
But the snail replied, "Too far, too far!" and gave a look
askance —
Said he thanked the whiting kindly, but he would not join
the dance.
Would not, could not, would not, could not, would not
join the dance.
Would not, could not, would not, could not, could not
join the dance.

"What matters it how far we go?" his scaly friend replied.
"There is another shore, you know, upon the other side.
The further off from England the nearer is to France —
Then turn not pale, beloved snail, but come and join the
      dance.
  Will you, won't you, will you, won't you, will you join
      the dance?
  Will you, won't you, will you, won't you, won't you join
      the dance?"

'TIS · CLEAR · ENOUGH · THE · ELEPHANT
IS · VERY · LIKE · A · TREE

III: METRICAL MEASURES

Rhythm in poetry depends upon the arrangement of accented and unaccented syllables. Between the accented syllables there are usually one or two unaccented syllables.

For give ness Lane is old as youth,
You can not miss your way.

This is the for est prim e val; the mur mur ing pines
and the hem locks

The rhythmic beats in these lines recur with such regularity that they are said to be metrical. The word "metrical" means measured. In prose the heavy accents do not fall at definite intervals, but are sometimes close together, sometimes far apart.

Alice was beginning to get very tired of sitting by her sister on the bank, and of having nothing to do.

Can your ear hear which of the following lines are metrical and which are not? If it can, then you have gone a long way in appreciating one of the chief differences between prose and poetry.

Animal crackers, and cocoa to drink,
That is the finest of suppers, I think;
When I'm grown up and can have what I please,
I think I shall always insist upon these.

Little crackers in animal shapes, and sweet cocoa to drink,
That is a good supper, I think;
When I am big and can eat everything I please,
I think I shall eat these.

There are four simple metrical patterns or units which are frequently used in English verse. Each unit is called a *foot*. The metrical pattern most often used is the *iambic* foot. It consists of an unaccented syllable followed by an accented syllable. For example: along; pretend; to go. If bars are set between metrical measures, as they are in music, the pattern of accents is easily seen.

Forgive | ness Lane | is old | as youth,

You can | not miss | your way;

'Tis hedged | with flow | ering thorn | forsooth,

Where white | doves fear | less stray.

The *trochaic* foot is the reverse of the iambic. It consists of an accented syllable followed by an unaccented one. For example: Henry; going; men and. Iambic meter moves more smoothly than trochaic meter, but the latter has greater strength and energy.

At the | door on | summer | even | ings

Sat the | little | Hia | watha;

Heard the | whispering | of the | pine trees

Heard the | lapping | of the | water.

The *anapestic* measure has two unaccented syllables followed by an accented one: interfere; to the end; in Japan. Anapestic lines have a swinging movement, like waves washing against the shore, or the long ripples the wind makes in a field of ripened grain.

[54]

The Ăssy̆r | iăn cáme dówn | líke thĕ wólf | ŏn thĕ fóld,

Ănd hĭs có | hŏrts wĕre gleám | ĭng ĭn púr | plĕ ănd góld;

Ănd thĕ sheén | ŏf theĭr speárs | wăs lĭke stárs | ŏn thĕ seá,

Whĕn thĕ blúe | wáve rólls níght | ly̆ ŏn deép | Gălĭleé.

The *dactylic* foot is made up of an accented syllable and two unaccented ones: át tĭ tŭde; ó vĕr thĕ; whĕre ĭn thĕ. Dactylic verses are especially effective in suggesting excitement and hurry.

Cánnŏn tŏ | ríght ŏf thĕm,

Cánnŏn tŏ | léft ŏf thĕm,

Cánnŏn ĭn | frónt ŏf thĕm

Vólleyĕd ănd | thúndĕrĕd.

A fifth kind of measure, the *spondee*, occurs occasionally within a line. The spondee consists of two accented syllables: góose stép; cóme, cóme!

No skillful poet ever follows his metrical pattern with monotonous regularity throughout a whole poem. He varies the pattern just enough to make the rhythm more interesting. Sometimes he omits a syllable; sometimes he adds one. Sometimes he begins an iambic line with a trochaic foot or drops a dactyl between two iambs. Sometimes, to secure the effect he desires, he may combine two patterns. However, he is always careful to keep the general pattern of his rhythm clear.

The skilled poet is like the skilled musician. Both can play old measures and make them sound fresh and new.

Lessons for a Boy

SAMUEL TAYLOR COLERIDGE

The boy who had his lessons in "metrical feet" from Coleridge must have found them easier to learn than names in geography. Can you guess why?

Trochee trips from long to short;
From long to long in solemn sort
Slow Spondee stalks; strong foot! yea ill able
Ever to come up with Dactyl trisyllable.
Iambics march from short to long; —
With a leap and a bound the swift Anapests throng.

The Blind Men and the Elephant

JOHN GODFREY SAXE

The meter of the poem resembles the opinions of the six men of Indostan —
somewhat "stiff and strong." The poem repeats a Hindoo fable.

It was six men of Indostan,
To learning much inclined,
Who went to see the Elephant
(Though all of them were blind),
That each by observation
Might satisfy his mind.

The First approached the Elephant,
And happening to fall
Against his broad and sturdy side,
At once began to bawl:
"God bless me! but the Elephant
Is very like a wall!"

The Second, feeling of the tusk,
Cried, "Ho! what have we here
So very round and smooth and sharp?
To me 'tis mighty clear
This wonder of an Elephant
Is very like a spear!"

The Third approached the animal,
And happening to take
The squirming trunk within his hands,
Thus boldly up and spake:
"I see," quoth he, "the Elephant
Is very like a snake!"

The Fourth reached out an eager hand,
   And felt about the knee:
"What most this wondrous beast is like
   Is mighty plain," quoth he;
"'Tis clear enough the Elephant
   Is very like a tree!"

The Fifth, who chanced to touch the ear,
   Said: "E'en the blindest man
Can tell what this resembles most;
   Deny the fact who can,
This marvel of an Elephant
   Is very like a fan!"

The Sixth no sooner had begun
   About the beast to grope,
Than, seizing on the swinging tail
   That fell within his scope,
"I see," quoth he, "the Elephant
   Is very like a rope!"

And so these men of Indostan
   Disputed loud and long,
Each in his own opinion
   Exceeding stiff and strong.
Though each was partly in the right
   They all were in the wrong!

The Mocking Bird and the Donkey

WILLIAM CULLEN BRYANT

This is a simple meter, and not very musical. But then, the donkey and the mock-bird were simple too, and not very musical!

A mock-bird in a village
Had somehow gained the skill
To imitate the voices
Of animals at will.

And singing in his prison,
Once, at the close of day,
He gave, with great precision,
The donkey's heavy bray.

Well pleased, the mock-bird's master
Sent to the neighbors round,
And bade them come together
To hear that curious sound.

They came, and all were talking
In praise of what they heard,
And one delighted lady
Would fain have bought the bird.

A donkey listened sadly,
And said: "Confess I must
That these are shallow people,
And terribly unjust.

"I'm bigger than the mock-bird,
And better bray than he,
Yet not a soul has uttered
A word in praise of me."

[59]

Forgiveness Lane

Martha Gilbert Dickinson

These iambic feet keep as even a pace as the steps of the friends who walk in pairs between the hedges of flowering thorn.

Forgiveness Lane is old as youth,
You cannot miss your way;
'Tis hedged with flowering thorn forsooth,
Where white doves fearless stray.

You must walk gently with your Love,
Frail blossoms dread your feet —
And bloomy branches close above
Make heaven near and sweet.

Some lovers fear the stile of pride
And turn away in pain —
But more have kissed where white doves hide
And blessed Forgiveness Lane!

The First Snowfall

JAMES RUSSELL LOWELL

So soft and even are these measures that their very sound helps you picture the noiseless fall of the snow.

The snow had begun in the gloaming,
　　And busily all the night
Had been heaping field and highway
　　With a silence deep and white.

Every pine and fir and hemlock
　　Wore ermine too dear for an earl,
And the poorest twig on the elm tree
　　Was ridged inch deep with pearl.

From sheds new-roofed with Carrara
　　Came Chanticleer's muffled crow,
The stiff rails softened to swan's-down,
　　And still fluttered down the snow.

I stood and watched by the window
　　The noiseless work of the sky,
And the sudden flurries of snowbirds
　　Like brown leaves whirling by.

I thought of a mound in sweet Auburn
　　Where a little headstone stood:
How the flakes were folding it gently,
　　As did robins the babes in the wood.

Up spoke our own little Mabel,
    Saying, "Father, who makes it snow?"
And I told of the good All-father
    Who cares for us here below.

Again I looked at the snowfall,
    And thought of the leaden sky
That arched o'er our first great sorrow,
    When that mound was heaped so high.

I remembered the gradual patience
    That fell from that cloud like snow,
Flake by flake, healing and hiding
    The scar that renewed our woe.

And again to the child I whispered,
    "The snow that husheth all,
Darling, the merciful Father
    Alone can make it fall!"

Then, with eyes that saw not, I kissed her;
    And she, kissing back, could not know
That my kiss was given to her sister,
    Folded close under deepening snow.

Firefly Song

HENRY WADSWORTH LONGFELLOW

The word "trochee" comes from a Greek word which means running foot. And indeed it seems as if these trochaic feet actually do run. The song is from "Hiawatha."

At the door on summer evenings
Sat the little Hiawatha;
Heard the whispering of the pine trees,
Heard the lapping of the water,
Sounds of music, words of wonder;
"Minne-wawa!" said the pine trees,
"Mudway-aushka!" said the water.
Saw the firefly, Wah-wah-taysee,
Flitting through the dusk of evening,
With the twinkle of its candle
Lighting up the brakes and bushes,
And he sang the song of children,
Sang the song Nokomis taught him:
"Wah-wah-taysee, little firefly,
Little, flitting, white-fire insect,
Little, dancing, white-fire creature,
Light me with your little candle,
Ere upon my bed I lay me,
Ere in sleep I close my eyelids!"

A Birthday

CHRISTINA ROSSETTI

The first stanza has a gentle, singing rhythm. In the second stanza, however, notice how the introduction of trochaic measures at the beginning of certain lines changes the rhythm. The trochees make the lines move faster and more forcefully.

My heart is like a singing bird
　　Whose nest is in a watered shoot:
My heart is like an apple tree
　　Whose boughs are bent with thick-set fruit.
My heart is like a rainbow shell
　　That paddles in a halcyon sea;
My heart is gladder than all these
　　Because my love is come to me.

Raise me a dais of silk and down;
　　Hang it with vair and purple dyes;
Carve it in doves and pomegranates,
　　And peacocks with a hundred eyes;
Work it in gold and silver grapes,
　　In leaves and silver fleurs-de-lys;
Because the birthday of my life
　　Is come, my love is come to me.

Vair is a species of squirrel fur, much used in olden times for the robes of royalty.

Animal Crackers

CHRISTOPHER MORLEY

Do you think the poet would use as zestful a meter as this to express the little boy's feeling for carrots and spinach?

Animal crackers, and cocoa to drink,
That is the finest of suppers, I think;
When I'm grown up and can have what I please,
I think I shall always insist upon these.

What do *you* choose when you're offered a treat? —
When Mother says, "What would you like best to eat?"
Is it waffles and syrup, or cinnamon toast?
It's cocoa and animals that I love the most!

The kitchen's the cosiest place that I know:
The kettle is singing, the stove is aglow,
And there in the twilight, how jolly to see
The cocoa and animals waiting for me.

Daddy and Mother dine later in state,
With Mary to cook for them, Susan to wait;
But they don't have nearly as much fun as I
Who eat in the kitchen with Nurse standing by;
And Daddy once said he would like to be me
Having cocoa and animals once more for tea!

Four Things

HENRY VAN DYKE

The firm, steady beat of the meter emphasizes the importance of what these two poets say.

Four things a man must learn to do
If he would make his record true:
To think without confusion clearly;
To love his fellow-men sincerely;
To act from honest motives purely;
To trust in God and Heaven securely.

The Character of a Happy Life

SIR HENRY WOTTON

How happy is he born and taught
That serveth not another's will;
Whose armor is his honest thought,
And simple truth his utmost skill!

This man is freed from servile bands
Of hope to rise or fear to fall:
Lord of himself, though not of lands,
And having nothing, yet hath all.

Columbus

Joaquin Miller

This meter has a sturdy beat, like the heart of courage that carried Columbus unswerving over shoreless seas to the light of dawn in a new world.

Behind him lay the gray Azores,
  Behind, the Gates of Hercules;
Before him not the ghost of shores,
  Before him only shoreless seas.
The good mate said: "Now must we pray,
  For lo! the very stars are gone.
Brave Admiral, speak; what shall I say?"
  "Why, say, 'Sail on! sail on! and on!'"

"My men grow mutinous day by day;
  My men grow ghastly wan and weak."
The stout mate thought of home; a spray
  Of salt wave washed his swarthy cheek.
"What shall I say, brave Admiral, say,
  If we sight naught but seas at dawn?"
"Why, you shall say at break of day:
  'Sail on! sail on! sail on! and on!'"

They sailed and sailed, as winds might blow,
  Until at last the blanched mate said:
"Why, now not even God would know
  Should I and all my men fall dead.
These very winds forget their way,
  For God from these dread seas is gone.
Now speak, brave Admiral, speak and say" —
  He said: "Sail on! sail on! and on!"

They sailed. They sailed. Then spake the mate:
  "This mad sea shows his teeth tonight.
He curls his lip, he lies in wait,
  With lifted teeth, as if to bite!
Brave Admiral, say but one good word:
  What shall we do when hope is gone?"
The words leapt like a leaping sword:
  "Sail on! sail on! sail on! and on!"

Then, pale and worn, he kept his deck,
  And peered through darkness. Ah, that night
Of all dark nights! And then a speck —
  A light! a light! a light! a light!
It grew, a starlit flag unfurled!
  It grew to be Time's burst of dawn.
He gained a world; he gave that world
  Its grandest lesson: "On! sail on!"

The Knight's Leap

CHARLES KINGSLEY

Two metrical measures are combined with stirring effect. Besieged, the Knight of Altenahr chooses to die rather than fall into the hands of his foes. Quickly he makes his decision; boldly he leaps to his death; and quick and bold is the meter.

So the foemen have fired the gate, men of mine,
   And the water is spent and gone?
Then bring me a cup of the red Ahr-wine:
   I never shall drink but this one:

"And reach me my harness, and saddle my horse,
   And lead him me round to the door:
He must take such a leap tonight perforce
   As horse never took before.

"I have fought my fight, I have lived my life,
   I have drunk my share of wine;
From Trier to Coln there was never a knight
   Led a merrier life than mine.

"I have lived by the saddle for years two score;
   And if I must die on tree,
Then the old saddle-tree, which has borne me of yore,
   Is the properest timber for me.

"So now to show Bishop, and burgher, and priest,
   How the Altenahr hawk can die;
If they smoke the old falcon out of his nest,
   He must take to his wings and fly!"

He harnessed himself by the clear moonshine,
  And he mounted his horse at the door;
And he drained such a cup of the red Ahr-wine
  As man never drained before.

He spurred the old horse, and he held him tight,
  And he leapt him out over the wall —
Out over the cliff, out into the night,
  Three hundred feet of fall.

They found him next morning below in the glen,
  With never a bone in him whole.
A mass or a prayer, now, good gentlemen,
  For such a bold rider's soul.

My Lost Youth

Henry Wadsworth Longfellow

The refrain which the poet remembers from an old song of his boyhood furnishes his metrical pattern.

Often I think of the beautiful town
　That is seated by the sea;
Often in thought go up and down
The pleasant streets of that dear old town,
　And my youth comes back to me.
　　And a verse of a Lapland song
　　Is haunting my memory still:
　　"A boy's will is the wind's will,
And the thoughts of youth are long, long thoughts."

I can see the shadowy lines of its trees,
　And catch, in sudden gleams,
The sheen of the far-surrounding seas,
And islands that were the Hesperides
　Of all my boyish dreams.
　　And the burden of that old song,
　　It murmurs and whispers still:
　　"A boy's will is the wind's will,
And the thoughts of youth are long, long thoughts."

I remember the black wharves and the slips,
　And the sea-tides tossing free;
And Spanish sailors with bearded lips,
And the beauty and mystery of the ships,
　And the magic of the sea.

And the voice of that wayward song
Is singing and saying still:
"A boy's will is the wind's will,
And the thoughts of youth are long, long thoughts."

I remember the bulwarks by the shore,
  And the fort upon the hill;
The sunrise gun, with its hollow roar,
The drumbeat repeated o'er and o'er,
  And the bugle wild and shrill,
    And the music of that old song
    Throbs in my memory still:
    "A boy's will is the wind's will,
And the thoughts of youth are long, long thoughts."

I remember the sea-fight far away,
  How it thundered o'er the tide!
And the dead captains, as they lay
In their graves, o'erlooking the tranquil bay
  Where they in battle died
    And the sound of that mournful song
    Goes through me with a thrill:
    "A boy's will is the wind's will,
And the thoughts of youth are long, long thoughts."

I can see the breezy dome of groves,
  The shadows of Deering's Woods;
And the friendships old and the early loves
Come back with a Sabbath sound, as of doves
  In quiet neighborhoods.
    And the verse of that sweet old song,
    It flutters and murmurs still:
    "A boy's will is the wind's will,
And the thoughts of youth are long, long thoughts."

I remember the gleams and glooms that dart,
  Across the schoolboy's brain;
The song and the silence in the heart,
That in part are prophecies, and in part
    Are longings wild and vain.
      And the voice of that fitful song
      Sings on, and is never still:
      "A boy's will is the wind's will,
And the thoughts of youth are long, long thoughts."

There are things of which I may not speak;
  There are dreams that cannot die;
There are thoughts that make the strong heart weak,
And bring a pallor into the cheek,
    And a mist before the eye.
      And the words of that fatal song
      Come over me like a chill:
      "A boy's will is the wind's will
And the thoughts of youth are long, long thoughts."

Strange to me now are the forms I meet
  When I visit the dear old town;
But the native air is pure and sweet,
And the trees that o'ershadow each well-known street,
    As they balance up and down,
      Are singing the beautiful song,
      Are sighing and whispering still:
      "A boy's will is the wind's will,
And the thoughts of youth are long, long thoughts."

And Deering's Woods are fresh and fair,
  And with joy that is almost pain
My heart goes back to wander there,

And among the dreams of the days that were,
　I find my lost youth again.
　　And the strange and beautiful song,
　　The groves are repeating it still:
　　"A boy's will is the wind's will,
And the thoughts of youth are long, long thoughts."

The *Hesperides* were the island gardens of the Sunset, where grew the golden apples of fable.　The country of one's dreams is often called the Hesperides.

Courage

GEORGE HERBERT

These are short lines, but how strong and vigorous!　The rhythm is as forthright as the courage which honesty requires.

Dare to be true;
　Nothing can need a lie;
The fault that needs one most
　Grows two thereby.

The Day Is Done

Henry Wadsworth Longfellow

A pensive mood expresses itself in a tranquil rhythm.   The poem would lose its flavor of sadness and longing if the words were set to a martial meter.

The day is done, and the darkness
  Falls from the wings of Night,
As a feather is wafted downward
  From an eagle in his flight.

I see the lights of the village
  Gleam through the rain and the mist,
And a feeling of sadness comes o'er me,
  That my soul cannot resist:

A feeling of sadness and longing,
  That is not akin to pain,
And resembles sorrow only
  As the mist resembles rain.

Come, read to me some poem,
  Some simple and heartfelt lay,
That shall soothe this restless feeling,
  And banish the thoughts of day.

Not from the grand old masters,
  Not from the bards sublime,
Whose distant footsteps echo
  Through the corridors of Time.

For, like strains of martial music,
    Their mighty thoughts suggest
Life's endless toil and endeavor;
    And tonight I long for rest.

Read from some humbler poet,
    Whose songs gushed from his heart,
As showers from the clouds of summer,
    Or tears from the eyelids start;

Who through long days of labor,
    And nights devoid of ease,
Still heard in his soul the music
    Of wonderful melodies.

Such songs have power to quiet
    The restless pulse of care,
And come like the benediction
    That follows after prayer.

Then read from the treasured volume
    The poem of thy choice,
And lend to the rhyme of the poet
    The music of thy voice.

And the night shall be filled with music,
    And the cares that infest the day
Shall fold their tents, like the Arabs,
    And as silently steal away.

Coronach

SIR WALTER SCOTT

The meter of this dirge, or coronach, echoes the rhythm of voices lifted in lament. Such a meter would not be sufficiently stately to represent the tolling of bells or a dirge played upon an organ.

He is gone on the mountain,
   He is lost in the forest,
Like a summer-dried fountain,
   When our need was the sorest.
The font, reappearing,
   From raindrops shall borrow,
But to us comes no cheering,
   To Duncan no morrow!

The hand of the reaper
   Takes the ears that are hoary,
But the voice of the weeper
   Wails manhood in glory.
The autumn winds rushing
   Waft the leaves that are serest,
But our flower was in flushing,
   When blighting was nearest.

Fleet foot on the corrie,
   Sage counsel in cumber,
Red hand in the foray,
   How sound is thy slumber!
Like the dew on the mountain,
   Like the foam on the river,
Like the bubble on the fountain,
   Thou art gone, and for ever.

The Destruction of Sennacherib

GEORGE NOEL GORDON, LORD BYRON

With gleaming banners and shining spears, wave upon wave, Sennacherib's armies sweep down to battle. And wave upon wave, as they sleep in the night, they perish from the pestilence that blows from the wings of the Angel of Death. Byron took his suggestion for the poem from the Bible, from the Second Book of the Kings, Chapter nineteen.

The Assyrian came down like the wolf on the fold,
And his cohorts were gleaming in purple and gold;
And the sheen of their spears was like stars on the sea,
When the blue wave rolls nightly on deep Galilee.

Like the leaves of the forest when Summer is green,
That host with their banners at sunset were seen:
Like the leaves of the forest when Autumn hath blown,
That host on the morrow lay withered and strown.

For the Angel of Death spread his wings on the blast,
And breathed in the face of the foe as he passed;
And the eyes of the sleepers waxed deadly and chill,
And their hearts but once heaved, and forever grew still!

And there lay the steed with his nostril all wide,
But through it there rolled not the breath of his pride:
And the foam of his gasping lay white on the turf,
And cold as the spray of the rock-beating surf.

And there lay the rider distorted and pale,
With the dew on his brow, and the rust on his mail;
And the tents were all silent, the banners alone,
The lances unlifted, the trumpet unblown.

And the widows of Ashur are loud in their wail,
And the idols are broke in the temple of Baal;
And the might of the Gentile, unsmote by the sword,
Hath melted like snow in the glance of the Lord!

Courage Has a Crimson Coat

NANCY BYRD TURNER

*Did it only happen so, or did the poet have a reason for making
each of the first six lines start off on a boldly accented syllable,
while the last two lines begin quietly?*

Courage has a crimson coat
   Trimmed with trappings bold,
Knowledge dons a dress of note,
   Fame's is cloth of gold.
Far they ride and fair they roam,
   Much they do and dare.
Gray-gowned Patience sits at home,
   And weaves the stuff they wear.

A Last Prayer

Helen Hunt Jackson

The accents in these lines fall softly and somewhat slowly. Can you see any reason why they should be neither loud nor fast?

Father, I scarcely dare to pray,
  So clear I see, now it is done,
That I have wasted half my day,
  And left my work but just begun;

So clear I see that things I thought
  Were right or harmless were a sin;
So clear I see that I have sought,
  Unconscious, selfish aims to win;

So clear I see that I have hurt
  The souls I might have helped to save;
That I have slothful been, inert,
  Deaf to the calls Thy leaders gave.

In outskirts of Thy kingdoms vast,
  Father, the humblest spot give me;
Set me the lowliest task Thou hast;
  Let me repentant work for Thee!

IV: IRREGULAR RHYTHMS

Not all poetry is metrical. The poetry of the Bible has rhythm, but no meter. The rhythm changes too much to conform to any fixed pattern. Read the lines aloud, and you find that your voice rises and falls in little waves of sound or cadences.

These cadences resemble one another, but they are not exactly alike. They vary in length. They vary in pitch too. The voice rises a little higher in some cadences than it does in others.

By the rivers of Babylon,   there we sat down,   yea,   we wept,
          when we remembered Zion.

We hanged our harps   upon the willows   in the midst thereof.

For there they   that carried us away captive   required of us a song;
          and they that wasted us   required of us mirth,
          saying,   Sing us one of the songs   of Zion.

How shall we sing   the Lord's song   in a strange land?

Ancient poets were not the only ones to build their verse upon cadence. Modern writers sometimes use it rather than meter. When they do, their writing is spoken of as free verse, because it is free from the strict arrangement of accents which metrical verse requires.

The rhythm of free verse is much the same as the rhythms of ordinary speech and of prose writing. The rhythm does not move by regular accents, but goes by irregular waves, sometimes long and sometimes short.

Now I tell   what my mother told me   today   as we sat
          at dinner together,

Of when she   was a nearly grown girl   living home with her parents
          on the old homestead.

Spring

So regular are these cadences that they seem almost metrical.   The poem is from the Old Testament.

F or, lo, the winter is past,
The rain is over and gone;
The flowers appear on the earth;
The time of the singing of birds is come,
And the voice of the turtle is heard in our land.

A SONG OF SOLOMON

The song of the *turtle-dove* is referred to in the last line.

What Is the Grass?

WALT WHITMAN

These lines seem to spread and be at ease, like the grass itself, taking no particular shape or pattern.   They are from "Song of Myself."

W hat is the grass?

I guess it must be the flag of my disposition, out of hopeful
        green stuff woven.
Or I guess it is the handkerchief of the Lord, dropped,
Bearing the owner's name someway in the corners, that we
        may see and remark and say "Whose?"
A scented gift and remembrancer designedly.

At a Window

Carl Sandburg

Especially in the second stanza the cadences are musical.   You will enjoy lingering over them as you read them aloud.

Give me hunger,
O you gods that sit and give
The world its orders.
Give me hunger, pain, and want;
Shut me out with shame and failure
From your doors of gold and fame,
Give me your shabbiest, weariest hunger.

But leave me a little love,
A voice to speak to me in the day end,
A hand to touch me in the dark room
Breaking the long loneliness.
In the dusk of day-shapes
Blurring the sunset,
One little wandering, western star
Thrust out from the changing shores of shadow.
Let me go to the window,
Watch there the day-shapes of dusk,
And wait and know the coming
Of a little love.

Clay Hills

JEAN STARR UNTERMEYER

Do you notice, as you read this poem, that when the poet is speaking of the yielding clay, her cadences are smoother and prettier than when she speaks of the stubborn rock?

It is easy to mould the yielding clay.
And many shapes grow into beauty
Under the facile hand.
But forms of clay are lightly broken;
They will lie shattered and forgotten in a dingy corner
But underneath the slipping clay
Is rock. . . .
I would rather work in stubborn rock
All the years of my life,
And make one strong thing
And set it in a high, clean place,
To recall the granite strength of my desire.

Wings

There is neither haste nor noisy whirring of wings in this smooth flight.   The lines are from the Fifty-fifth Psalm in the Bible.

O that I had wings like a dove!
For then would I fly away and be at rest.
Lo, then would I wander far off,
And remain in the wilderness.

A SONG OF DAVID

As Toilsome I Wandered Virginia's Woods

Walt Whitman

The shuffling of feet through fallen leaves and the quick, sharp march of soldiers are both to be heard in these rhythms.

As toilsome I wandered Virginia's woods,
To the music of rustling leaves kicked by my feet (for 'twas
      autumn),
I marked at the foot of a tree the grave of a soldier;
Mortally wounded he and buried on the retreat (easily all
      could I understand),
The halt of a midday hour, when up! no time to lose —
      yet this sign left,
On a tablet scrawled and nailed on the tree by the grave,
Bold, cautious, true, and my loving comrade.

Long, long I muse, then on my way go wandering,
Many a changeful season to follow, and many a scene of life,
Yet at times through changeful season and scene, abrupt,
      alone, or in the crowded street,
Comes before me the unknown soldier's grave, comes the
      inscription rude in Virginia's woods,
Bold, cautious, true, and my loving comrade.

O Captain! My Captain

Walt Whitman

The poet's grief over the death of Lincoln expresses itself in cadences so stately that they are almost metrical.

O Captain! my Captain! our fearful trip is done,
The ship has weathered every rack, the prize we sought is
    won,
The port is near, the bells I hear, the people all exulting,
While follow eyes the steady keel, the vessel grim and
    daring;
        But O heart! heart! heart!
          O the bleeding drops of red,
        Where on the deck my Captain lies
          Fallen cold and dead.

O Captain! my Captain! rise up and hear the bells;
Rise up — for you the flag is flung — for you the bugle
    trills,
For you bouquets and ribboned wreaths — for you the shores
    a-crowding,
For you they call, the swaying mass, their eager faces
    turning;
        Here Captain! dear father!
          This arm beneath your head!
        It is some dream that on the deck
          You've fallen cold and dead.

My Captain does not answer, his lips are pale and still,
My father does not feel my arm, he has no pulse nor will,
The ship is anchored safe and sound, its voyage closed and
      done,
From fearful trip the victor ship comes in with object won;
      Exult O shores, and ring O bells!
        But I with mournful tread,
       Walk the deck my Captain lies,
        Fallen cold and dead.

The Leader

These verses owe their stately grace as much to their rhythm as to their meaning. They are taken from the Second Book of Samuel in the Bible.

He that ruleth over men must be just,
Ruling in the fear of God.
And he shall be as the light of the morning,
      when the sun riseth;
Even a morning without clouds;
As the tender grass springing out of the earth,
By clear shining after rain.

TILL · 'MID · LAUGHTER · A · SHIELD · WAS
LEVELED · AND · VIGI · RODE · ON · IT

V: Length of Line

A poet is sometimes spoken of as an architect of verse. The architect translates steel and brick and stone into shapely buildings, into churches and towering skyscrapers. The materials with which the poet works are words. His buildings are poems.

Compared with the structures which the architect rears, a poem is a very slight thing indeed. Yet it may outlast thick walls of stone. Long, long centuries ago the palaces and towered battlements of Troy crumbled to dusty ruin, but the verses which the poet built to celebrate their splendor still stand as fair as on the day when first they took shape. Time has destroyed the citadel of Troy, but poetry preserves forever its glory and its beauty.

Since poetry, like architecture, takes definite shape and line, it is not surprising that the poet builds according to a definite plan. He measures his verses, although he does not use compass and ruler. He measures by counting the number of metrical feet, to make sure that his verses are all of the proper length. (A verse is a line of poetry.) The following verses contain respectively four, three, and two feet.

The chief | defect | of Hen | ry King	4
Was chew | ing lit | tle bits | of string.	4
As a beau | ty I'm not | a great star,	3
There are oth | ers more hand | some by far.	3
Cannon to | right of them,	2
Cannon to | left of them.	2

The length of line is not determined by how long it looks on the page. These two verses are of the same metrical length, although one looks shorter than the other.

They gave | him Tea | and cakes | and Jam   4
And sli | ces of | deli | cious Ham.   4

Sometimes the lines of a poem are all of the same length. Sometimes, for the sake of variety, they are of different lengths. Notice, however, that long and short lines do not follow each other in haphazard order. They are arranged according to some definite pattern or plan. Notice also that the lines are indented to help the eye catch the rhymes and see the order of arrangement of long lines and short.

We walked | along, | while bright | and red   4
Uprose | the morn | ing sun;   3
And Mat | thew stopped, | he looked, | and said,   4
"The will | of God | be done!"   3

"O Ma | ry, go | and call | the cat | tle home,   5
And call | the cat | tle home,   3
And call | the cat | tle home   3
Across | the sands | of Dee;"   3
The west | ern wind | was wild | and dank | with foam,   5
And all | alone | went she.   3

English poetry uses lines ranging from one to eight feet, but verses of three, four, and five measures are most frequently used. Lines which consist of one or two feet seem rather short and jerky for the expression of dignified ideas. On the other hand, if lines are too long, it is difficult for the ear to detect the rhythmic pattern.

Verses are described according to the number of feet they contain. The Greek numerals are added to the word *meter*, meaning measure (which comes from the Greek), to name the lines: *monometer*, one foot; *dimeter*, two feet;

trimeter, three feet;   *tetrameter*, four feet;   *pentameter*, five feet;
hexameter, six feet;   *septameter*, seven feet;   *octameter*, eight feet.

To indicate the pattern of a line, one must tell both the name of the prevailing foot and the number of feet in the line.

Obey | thy heart.   *Iambic dimeter*

This   is   the | forest   pri | meval.   The | murmuring | pines   and   the |
     hemlocks   *Dactylic   hexameter*

Rolled   to | starboard, | rolled   to | larboard, | when   the | surge   was |
     seething | free.   *Trochaic octameter*

Long lines, like long processions, move more slowly than short ones.   For this reason they give an impression of weight and dignity.   Sometimes a humorous verse maker takes advantage of this fact.   He clothes an amusing idea in a fine, long, rolling line, and the effect is much like that of a small boy dressed up in his father's flapping shoes and bagging trousers.

Time, You Old Gipsy Man

Ralph Hodgson

Gipsy Time is no loiterer.   Tirelessly he pushes forward on his swift steed, from century to century.   The short lines suggest how momentary a hundred years must seem to him.

Time, you old gipsy man,
Will you not stay,
Put up your caravan
Just for one day?

All things I'll give you,
Will you be my guest,
Bells for your jennet
Of silver the best,
Goldsmiths shall beat you
A great golden ring,
Peacocks shall bow to you,
Little boys sing.
Oh, and sweet girls will
Festoon you with May.
Time, you old gipsy,
Why hasten away?

Last week in Babylon,
Last night in Rome,
Morning, and in the crush
Under Paul's dome;
Under Paul's dial
You tighten your rein —

Only a moment,
And off once again;
Off to some city
Now blind in the womb,
Off to another
Ere that's in the tomb.

Time, you old gipsy man,
Will you not stay,
Put up your caravan
Just for one day?

Time is pictured as riding a small Spanish horse, a *jennet,* and festooned with *May* (English hawthorn blossoms). *Under Paul's dome* refers to St. Paul's Cathedral in London.

Every Day

FELIX MENDELSSOHN

The motto for Every Day is more compelling because of its brisk, brief rhythms.

Love the beautiful,
Seek out the true,
Wish for the good,
And the best do!

Vigi

KATHARINE LEE BATES

Do you think that septameters would be as suitable for a poodle as they are for the tawny Irish Vigi?

Wisest of dogs was Vigi, a tawny-coated hound
That King Olaf, warring over green hills of Ireland,
    found;
His merry Norse were driving away a mighty herd
For feasts upon the dragon-ships, when an isleman dared
    a word:

"From all those stolen hundreds, well might ye spare my
    score."
"Aye, take them," quoth the gamesome king, "but not a
    heifer more.
Choose out thine own, nor hinder us; yet choose without a
    slip."
The isleman laughed and whistled, his finger at his lip.

Oh, swift the bright-eyed Vigi went darting through the
    herd
And singled out his master's neat with a nose that never
    erred,
And drave the star-marked twenty forth, to the wonder of
    the king,
Who bought the hound right honestly, at the price of a
    broad gold ring.

If the herd-dog dreamed of an Irish voice and of cattle on
      the hill,
He told it not to Olaf the King, whose will was Vigi's will,
But followed him far in faithful love and bravely helped
      him win
His famous fight with Thorir Hart and Raud, the wizard
      Finn.

Above the clamor and the clang shrill sounded Vigi's bark,
And when the groaning ship of Raud drew seaward to the
      dark,
And Thorir Hart leapt to the land, bidding his rowers live
Who could, Olaf and Vigi strained hard on the fugitive.

'Twas Vigi caught the runner's heel and stayed the wind-
      swift flight
Till Olaf's well-hurled spear had changed the day to endless
      night
For Thorir Hart, but not before his sword had stung the
      hound,
Whom the heroes bore on shield to ship, all grieving for his
      wound.

Now proud of heart was Vigi to be borne to ship on shield,
And many a day thereafter, when the bitter thrust was
      healed,
Would the dog leap up on the Vikings and coax with his
      Irish wit
Till 'mid laughter a shield was leveled, and Vigi rode on it.

America for Me

HENRY VAN DYKE

Long lines seem appropriate for suggesting long distances. It is a happy traveler who speaks; that you can tell by the lilt of the rhythm.

T is fine to see the Old World, and travel up and down
Among the famous palaces and cities of renown,
To admire the crumbly castles and the statues of the kings, —
But now I think I've had enough of antiquated things.

> So it's home again, and home again, America for me!
> My heart is turning home again, and there I long to be,
> In the land of youth and freedom beyond the ocean
>   bars,
> Where the air is full of sunlight and the flag is full of
>   stars.

Oh, London is a man's town, there's power in the air;
And Paris is a woman's town, with flowers in her hair;
And it's sweet to dream in Venice, and it's great to study
            Rome;
But when it comes to living, there is no place like home.

I like the German fir-woods, in green battalions drilled;
I like the gardens of Versailles with flashing fountains filled;
But, oh, to take your hand, my dear, and ramble for a day
In the friendly western woodland where Nature has her
            way!

I know that Europe's wonderful, yet something seems to
            lack:
The Past is too much with her, and the people looking back.

But the glory of the Present is to make the Future free, —
We love our land for what she is and what she is to be.

> Oh, it's home again, and home again, America for me!
> I want a ship that's westward bound to plow the rolling
> sea,
> To the blessed Land of Room Enough beyond the
> ocean bars,
> Where the air is full of sunlight and the flag is full of
> stars.

In the Forest

Henry Wadsworth Longfellow

*There is something of nobility in the movement of these verses from the
Prelude of "Evangeline," — the nobility of forests and deep-gliding rivers
and long-enduring love.*

This is the forest primeval.   The murmuring pines and
the hemlocks,
Bearded with moss, and in garments green, indistinct in the
twilight,
Stand like Druids of eld, with voices sad and prophetic;
Stand like harpers hoar, with beards that rest on their
bosoms.
Loud from its rocky caverns, the deep-voiced neighboring
ocean
Speaks, and in accents disconsolate answers the wail of the
forest.

This is the forest primeval; but where are the hearts that
   beneath it
Leaped like the roe, when he hears in the woodland the
   voice of the huntsman?
Where is the thatch-roofed village, the home of Acadian
   farmers —
Men whose lives glided on like rivers that water the wood-
   lands,
Darkened by shadows of earth, but reflecting an image of
   heaven?
Waste are those pleasant farms, and the farmers forever
   , departed!
Scattered like dust and leaves, when the mighty blasts of
   October .
Seize them, and whirl them aloft, and sprinkle them far o'er
   the ocean.
Naught but tradition remains of the beautiful village of
   Grand-Pré.

Ye who believe in affection that hopes, and endures, and
   is patient,
Ye who believe in the beauty and strength of woman's
   devotion,
List to the mournful tradition still sung by the pines of the
   forest;
List to a Tale of Love in Acadie, home of the happy.

The Glove and the Lions

Leigh Hunt

These are long lines, but the nobles and the ladies of King Francis' court were accustomed to pomp and dignity.

King Francis was a hearty king, and loved a royal sport,
And one day, as his lions fought, sat looking on the court;
The nobles filled the benches, and the ladies in their pride,
And 'mongst them sat the Count de Lorge, with one for
    whom he sighed;
And truly 'twas a gallant thing to see that crowning show —
Valor and love, and a king above, and the royal beasts
    below.

Ramped and roared the lions, with horrid, laughing jaws;
They bit, they glared, gave blows like beams, a wind went
    with their paws;
With wallowing might and stifled roar they rolled on one
    another,
Till all the pit, with sand and mane, was in a thunderous
    smother;
The bloody foam above the bars came whisking through the
    air;
Said Francis then, "Faith, gentlemen, we're better here
    than there!"

De Lorge's love o'erheard the king, a beauteous, lively
    dame,
With smiling lips, and sharp, bright eyes, which always
    seemed the same;

She thought, "The Count, my lover, is as brave as brave
     can be;
He surely would do wondrous things to show his love of me;
King, ladies, lovers, all look on; the occasion is divine;
I'll drop my glove to prove his love; great glory will be
     mine."

She dropped her glove to prove his love, then looked at
     him and smiled;
He bowed and in a moment leaped among the lions wild:
The leap was quick; return was quick; he has regained his
     place,
Then threw the glove, but not with love, right in the lady's
     face!
"By Heaven," said Francis, "rightly done!" and he rose
     from where he sat;
"No love," quoth he, "but vanity, sets love a task like that."

Upon His Departure Hence

ROBERT HERRICK

*This is one of the very few poems in the English language which
are written entirely in monometer.*

Thus I
Pass by
And die
As one
Unknown
And gone.

Song

CHRISTINA ROSSETTI

*The poet would not have grief drag its dark length across the life
of him she loves. Therefore she sings of her going, a song gentle
and sweet as April showers in a quiet wood.*

When I am dead, my dearest,
 Sing no sad songs for me;
Plant thou no roses at my head,
 Nor shady cypress tree:
Be the green grass above me
 With showers and dewdrops wet;
And if thou wilt, remember,
 And if thou wilt, forget.

I shall not see the shadows,
 I shall not feel the rain;
I shall not hear the nightingale
 Sing on, as if in pain:
And dreaming through the twilight
 That doth not rise nor set,
Haply I may remember
 And haply may forget.

Small and Early

Tudor Jenks

*Dorothy's father enters into the spirit of the little girl's "make-believe"
by dressing his description of her party in long, dignified-looking verses.*

When Dorothy and I took tea, we sat upon the floor;
No matter how much tea I drank, she always gave me more;
Our table was the scarlet box in which her teaset came;
Our guests, an armless one-eyed doll, a wooden horse gone
    lame.
She poured out nothing, very fast — the teapot tipped on
    high —
And in the bowl found sugar lumps unseen by my dull eye.
She added rich (pretended) cream — it seemed a willful
    waste,
For though she overflowed the cup, it did not change the
    taste.
She asked, "Take milk?" or "Sugar?" and though I
    answered, "No,"
She put them in and told me that I "must take it so!"
She'd say, "Another cup, Papa?" and I, "No, thank you,
    Ma'am,"
But then I had to take it — her courtesy was sham.
Still, being neither green, nor black, nor English breakfast
    tea,
It did not give her guests the "nerves" — whatever those
    may be.
Though often I upset my cup, she only minded when
I would mistake the empty cups for those she'd filled again.
She tasted my cup gingerly, for fear I'd burn my tongue;

Indeed, she really hurt my pride — she made me feel so
    young.
I must have drunk some twoscore cups, and Dorothy
    sixteen,
Allowing only needful time to pour them in between.
We stirred with massive pewter spoons and sipped in courtly
    ease,
With all the ceremony of the stately Japanese.
At length she put the cups away. "Goodnight, Papa,"
    she said:
And I went to a real tea, and Dorothy to bed.

A Swing Song

William Allingham

*Short and long, long and short, these lines mark the rhythm to
which the little boy swings care-free through the summer air.*

Swing, swing,
    Sing, sing,
Here! my throne and I am a king!
    Swing, sing,
    Swing, sing,
Farewell, earth, for I'm on the wing!

    Low, high,
    Here I fly,
Like a bird through sunny sky;
    Free, free,
    Over the lea,
Over the mountain, over the sea!

Up, down,
Up and down,
Which is the way to London Town?
Where?   Where?
Up in the air,
Close your eyes, and now you are there!

Soon, soon,
Afternoon,
Over the sunset, over the moon;
Far, far,
Over all bar,
Sweeping on from star to star!

No, no,
Low, low,
Sweeping daisies with my toe.
Slow, slow,
To and fro,
Slow —
slow —
slow —
slow.

In School Days

John Greenleaf Whittier

Neither too long nor too short, the alternating iambic tetrameter and trimeter are well suited to tell a story of school days.

Still sits the schoolhouse by the road,
    A ragged beggar sunning;
Around it still the sumacs grow,
    And blackberry vines are running.

Within, the master's desk is seen,
    Deep scarred by raps official;
The warping floor, the battered seats,
    The jackknife's carved initial;

The charcoal frescoes on its wall;
    Its door's worn sill, betraying
The feet that, creeping slow to school,
    Went storming out to playing!

Long years ago a winter sun
    Shone over it at setting;
Lit up its western windowpanes,
    And low eaves' icy fretting.

It touched the tangled golden curls,
    And brown eyes full of grieving,
Of one who still her steps delayed
    When all the school were leaving.

For near her stood the little boy
   Her childish favor singled:
His cap pulled low upon a face
   Where pride and shame were mingled.

Pushing with restless feet the snow
   To right and left, he lingered; —
As restlessly her tiny hands
   The blue-checked apron fingered.

He saw her lift her eyes; he felt
   The soft hand's light caressing,
And heard the tremble of her voice,
   As if a fault confessing.

"I'm sorry that I spelt the word:
   I hate to go above you,
Because" — the brown eyes lower fell —
   "Because, you see, I love you!"

Still memory to a gray-haired man
   That sweet child-face is showing.
Dear girl! the grasses on her grave
   Have forty years been growing!

He lives to learn, in life's hard school,
   How few who pass above him
Lament their triumph and his loss,
   Like her — because they love him.

The Duke of Plaza-Toro

W. S. GILBERT

Not a very warlike rhythm, this!   And yet the Duke of Plaza-Toro led his regiment!

In enterprise of martial kind,
  When there was any fighting,
He led his regiment from behind —
  He found it less exciting.

But when away his regiment ran,
  His place was at the fore, O —
    That celebrated,
    Cultivated,
    Underrated
      Nobleman,
  The Duke of Plaza-Toro!

In the first and foremost flight, ha, ha!
You always found that knight, ha, ha!
    That celebrated,
    Cultivated,
    Underrated
      Nobleman,
  The Duke of Plaza-Toro!

When, to evade Destruction's hand,
  To hide they all proceeded,
No soldier in that gallant band
  Hid half as well as he did.

He lay concealed throughout the war,
And so preserved his gore, O!
That unaffected,
Undetected,
Well-connected
Warrior,
The Duke of Plaza-Toro!

In every doughty deed, ha, ha!
He always took the lead, ha, ha!
That unaffected,
Undetected,
Well-connected
Warrior,
The Duke of Plaza-Toro!

Sir Bailey Barre

W. S. GILBERT

A pompous, strutting fellow is Sir Bailey Barre. Wouldn't he have been annoyed if the verse maker had used little short lines to describe him? . . . How would you like to employ Sir Bailey as your lawyer?

A complicated gentleman allow me to present,
Of all the arts and faculties the terse embodiment,
He's a great Arithmetician who can demonstrate with ease
That two and two are three, or five, or anything you please;
An eminent Logician who can make it clear to you
That black is white — when looked at from the proper point
of view;
A marvelous Philologist who'll undertake to show
That "yes" is but another and a neater form of "no."

The Mouse

ELIZABETH COATSWORTH

Would the plaint of the mouse be as mouse-y if it were expressed in long, slow-moving lines?

I hear a mouse
Bitterly complaining
In a crack of moonlight
Aslant on the floor —

"Little I ask
And that little is not granted.
There are few crumbs
In this world any more.

"The bread box is tin
And I cannot get in.

"The jam's in a jar
My teeth cannot mar.

"The cheese sits by itself
On the pantry shelf. —

"All night I run
Searching and seeking,
All night I run
About on the floor.

"Moonlight is there
And a bare place for dancing,
But no little feast
Is spread any more."

The Chameleon

A. P. HERBERT

The chameleon changes color; the child's thoughts and wishes change shape.

The chameleon changes his color;
　　He can look like a tree or a wall;
He is timid and shy and he hates to be seen,
So he simply sits down on the grass and grows green,
　　And pretends he is nothing at all.

I wish I could change my complexion
　　To purple or orange or red:
I wish I could look like the arm of a chair
So nobody ever would know I was there
　　When they wanted to put me to bed.

I wish I could be a chameleon
　　And look like a lily or rose;
I'd lie on the apples and peaches and pears,
But not on Aunt Margaret's yellowy chairs —
　　I should have to be careful of those.

The chameleon's life is confusing;
　　He is used to adventure and pain;
But if ever he sat on Aunt Maggie's cretonne
And found what a curious color he'd gone,
　　I don't think he'd do it again.

VI: RHYME

If all the rhyming words were taken out of the language, how much of its charm would be lost! There would be no Mother Goose to delight the youngest children. There would be no counting-out to settle who is to be "it" in hide-and-seek.

> Eeny, meeny, miney, mo,
> Catch a badger by the toe;
> If he hollers, let him go,
> Eeny, meeny, miney, *mo!*

If there were no rhymes, who would ever make a wish on a creaking load of hay or the first pale star of evening?

> Star light, star bright,
> First star I see tonight,
> Wish I may, wish I might
> Have the wish I wish tonight.

Or what little girl in play would count buttons on a dress or the silver-white petals of a daisy to find what husband she is to wed?

> Rich man, poor man, beggarman, thief,
> Doctor, lawyer, merchant, chief!

There would be less fun in the world too, if rhymes disappeared. Christopher Robin could not again have "sneezles and wheezles," although he might have the measles. The Rinktum-Winktum of Hindustan, that

> most polite and elegant man,
> With a nose that spread like the end of a fan,

would have to yield his title, his nose, and his kingdom when he gave up the rhyming words that named them.

No more nonsense verses would amuse the ear.

> A centipede was happy quite,
>   Until a frog, in fun,
> Said, "Pray, which leg comes after which?"
> This raised her mind to such a pitch
> She lay distracted in a ditch,
>   Considering how to run.

Not only something of pleasure and gayety but a quality of beauty would be forever lost if there were no words to rhyme. We should be poor, indeed, without the lovely rhyming lines which poets have wrought.

> Now fades the glimmering landscape on the sight,
>   And all the air a solemn stillness holds,
> Save where the beetle wheels his droning flight,
>   And drowsy tinklings lull the distant folds.

The dictionary defines rhyme as similarity of sound between words. The simplest rhymes are rhymes of one syllable: *go, toe, though; smile*, croco*dile; float, boat*, anti*dote*. The spelling does not matter. *Way* and in*veigh* are similar in sound though they differ in spelling. Rhymes of one syllable are called single rhymes or masculine rhymes.

Two-syllable rhymes are called double or feminine rhymes: *eeny, meeny; gleaming*, re*deeming*, unbe*seeming; shepherd, leopard; station*, cru*stacean; sing now, bring now, cling now*. Double rhymes often give a smooth, flowing movement to the verses.

> Where the copsewood is the greenest,
> Where the fountains glisten sheenest,
> Where the lady-fern grows strongest,
> Where the morning dew lies longest,
> Where the black-cock sweetest sips it,
> Where the fairy latest trips it.

Some rhymes are of more than two syllables: *quality,* fri*volity;* a*bility,* frag*ility,* versa*tility; best of it, rest of it, crest* *of it.* All rhymes of more than one syllable are called polysyllabic (many-syllabled) rhymes. They are often used for a humorous effect.

> O ye lords of ladies intellectual,
> Inform us truly, have they not henpecked you all?

Usually rhyme occurs at the end of lines, as in the couplet quoted above. Sometimes, however, a word or words within the line rhyme with the end of the line. This is called internal rhyme, to distinguish it from end rhyme.

"Be that word our sign of parting, bird or fiend!" I shrieked, upstarting:
"Get thee back into the tempest and the Night's Plutonian shore!
Leave no black plume as a token of that lie thy soul hath spoken!
Leave my loneliness unbroken! quit the bust above my door!"

Rhyme is not essential to poetry. Shakespeare and Milton, two of the greatest poets who ever lived, did not always use it. Nor, on the other hand, is everything that rhymes worthy of the name of poetry. It may be amusing nonsense verse or merely doggerel. In the hands of the true poet, however, rhyme becomes an adornment.

Placed at the end of the line, rhyme helps to mark the rhythmic pattern. Rhymes may occur in couplets.

> She was a phantom of delight   *a*
> When first she gleamed upon my sight.   *a*

Frequently, alternate lines rhyme, and the verses seem then to be interlocked by keys of chiming sound.

> Over the mountains   *a*
> And over the waves,   *b*
> Under the fountains   *a*
> And under the graves;   *b*
> Under floods that are deepest,   *c*
> Which Neptune obey,   *d*
> Over rocks that are steepest,   *c*
> Love will find out the way.   *d*

[113]

The poet may weave an intricate pattern, linking line with line by the interwoven music of his rhymes.

Swiftly walk o'er the western wave,	*a*
Spirit of Night!	*b*
Out of the misty eastern cave,	*a*
Where, all the long and lone daylight,	*b*
Thou wovest dreams of joy and fear,	*c*
Which make thee terrible and dear —	*c*
Swift be thy flight!	*b*

Poetry is written to be read aloud, for the music of rhythm and rhyme. As you read it, listen for the recurring echo of the rhymes, like notes of music repeated or chimes of bells played in tune.

Little Giffen

Francis O. Ticknor

The language of the poem and the rhymes are sharp and terse, as becomes so dramatic and brief a story.

Out of the focal and foremost fire,
Out of the hospital walls as dire,
Smitten of grapeshot and gangrene
(Eighteenth battle, and he sixteen!) —
Specter such as you seldom see,
Little Giffen of Tennessee.

"Take him and welcome!" the surgeons said;
"Little the doctor can help the dead!"
So we took him; and brought him where
The balm was sweet in the summer air;
And we laid him down on a wholesome bed —
Utter Lazarus, heel to head!

And we watched the war with bated breath —
Skeleton Boy against skeleton Death.
Months of torture, how many such!
Weary weeks of the stick and crutch;
And still a glint of the steel-blue eye
Told of a spirit that wouldn't die, —

And didn't. Nay, more! in death's despite
The crippled skeleton learned to write.
"Dear Mother," at first, of course; and then
"Dear Captain," inquiring about the men.
Captain's answer: "Of eighty and five,
Giffen and I are left alive."

Word of gloom from the war, one day:
"Johnston's pressed at the front, they say."
Little Giffen was up and away;
A tear — his first — as he bade good-by,
Dimmed the glint of his steel-blue eye.
"I'll write, if spared!"   There was news of the fight;
But none of Giffen. — He did not write.

I sometimes fancy that, were I king
Of the princely Knights of the Golden Ring,
With the song of the minstrel in mine ear,
And the tender legend that trembles here,
I'd give the best on his bended knee,
The whitest soul of my chivalry,
For Little Giffen of Tennessee.

Lazarus, in the Bible story, lay at the rich man's gate, full of sores.
The Knights of the Golden Ring were King Arthur's Knights of the Round
Table.

The Knight's Toast

Notice how skillfully the poet intertwines the rhymes within each stanza.

The feast is o'er! Now brimming wine
In lordly cup is seen to shine
  Before each eager guest;
And silence fills the crowded hall,
As deep as when the herald's call
  Thrills in the loyal breast.

Then up arose the noble host
And smiling cried: "A toast! a toast!
  To all our ladies fair!
Here, before all, I pledge the name
Of Staunton's proud and beauteous dame —
  The lady Gundamere!"

Then to his feet each gallant sprung,
And joyous was the shout that rung,
  As Stanley gave the word;
And every cup was raised on high,
Nor ceased the loud and gladsome cry,
  Till Stanley's voice was heard.

"Enough, enough," he smiling said,
And lowly bent his haughty head;
  "That all may have their due,
Now each in turn must play his part,
And pledge the lady of his heart,
  Like gallant knight and true!"

Then one by one each guest sprung up,
And drained in turn the brimming cup,
  And named the loved one's name;
And each, as hand on high he raised,
His lady's grace or beauty praised,
  Her constancy and fame.

'Tis now St. Leon's turn to rise;
On him are fixed those countless eyes;
  A gallant knight is he;
Envied by some, admired by all,
Far-famed in lady's bower and hall —
  The flower of chivalry.

St. Leon raised his kindling eye,
And lifts the sparkling cup on high;
  "I drink to one," he said,
"Whose image never may depart,
Deep graven on this grateful heart,
  Till memory be dead.

"To one whose love for me shall last
When lighter passions long have passed,
  So holy 'tis and true;
To one whose love hath longer dwelt,
More deeply fixed, more keenly felt,
  Than any pledged by you!"

Each guest upstarted at the word,
And laid a hand upon his sword,
  With fury-flashing eye;
And Stanley said: "We crave the name,
Proud knight, of this most peerless dame,
  Whose love you count so high."

St. Leon paused, as if he would
Not breathe her name in careless mood,
   Thus, lightly, to another;
Then bent his noble head, as though
To give the word the reverence due,
   And gently said: "My Mother!"

Attributed to SIR WALTER SCOTT

Patriotism

SIR WALTER SCOTT

Like the steady strokes of a hammer are these firm rhymes.

Breathes there the man, with soul so dead,
Who never to himself hath said,
   "This is my own, my native land!"
Whose heart hath ne'er within him burned
As home his footsteps he hath turned
   From wandering on a foreign strand?
If such there breathe, go, mark him well;
For him no minstrel raptures swell;
High though his titles, proud his name,
Boundless his wealth as wish can claim;
Despite those titles, power, and pelf,
The wretch, concentered all in self,
Living, shall forfeit fair renown,
And, doubly dying, shall go down
To the vile dust from whence he sprung,
Unwept, unhonored, and unsung.

Love Will Find Out the Way

The short trochaic lines and the double rhyming give these stanzas almost a flying movement. Is it appropriate to the thought?

Over the mountains
　And over the waves,
Under the fountains
　And under the graves;
Under floods that are deepest,
　Which Neptune obey,
Over rocks that are steepest,
　Love will find out the way.

When there is no place
　For the glowworm to lie,
When there is no space
　For receipt of a fly;
When the midge dares not venture
　Lest herself fast she lay,
If Love come, he will enter
　And will find out the way.

You may esteem him
　A child for his might;
Or you may deem him
　A coward for his flight;
But if she whom Love doth honor
　Be concealed from the day,
Set a thousand guards upon her,
　Love will find out the way.

Some think to lose him
    By having him confined;
And some do suppose him,
    Poor heart! to be blind;
But if ne'er so close ye wall him,
    Do the best that ye may,
Blind Love, if so ye call him,
    He will find out the way.

If the earth it should part him,
    He would gallop it o'er;
If the seas should o'erthwart him,
    He would swim to the shore;
Should his Love become a swallow,
    Through the air to stray,
Love will lend wings to follow,
    And will find out the way.

There is no striving
    To cross his intent;
There is no contriving
    His plots to prevent;
But if once the message greet him
    That his True Love doth stay,
If Death should come and meet him,
    Love will find out the way!

ANONYMOUS

Morning Song

KARLE WILSON BAKER

These triplet rhymes of the "Morning Song" sing their way into your very heart.

There's a mellower light just over the hill,
And somewhere a yellower daffodil,
And honey, somewhere, that's sweeter still.

And some were meant to stay like a stone,
Knowing the things they have always known,
Sinking down deeper into their own;

But some must follow the wind and me,
Who like to be starting and like to be free,
Never so glad as we're going to be!

The Vagabonds

John Townsend Trowbridge

If their story had not been told in verse, faithful Roger and his master would long ago have been forgotten. Rhyme and meter have made the two vagabonds memorable.

We are two travelers, Roger and I.
  Roger's my dog. — Come here, you scamp!
Jump for the gentleman — mind your eye!
  Over the table; look out for the lamp! —
The rogue is growing a little old;
  Five years we've trampled through wind and weather,
And slept outdoors when nights were cold,
  And ate and drank — and starved — together.

We've learned what comfort is, I tell you!
  A bed on the floor, a bit of rosin,
A fire to thaw our thumbs (poor fellow!
  The paw he holds up there's been frozen),
Plenty of catgut for my fiddle
  (This outdoor business is bad for strings),
Then a few nice buckwheats hot from the griddle,
  And Roger and I set up for kings.

No, thank ye, sir; I never drink;
  Roger and I are exceedingly moral —
Aren't we, Roger? — See him wink! —
  Well, something hot, then; we won't quarrel.
He's thirsty too — see him nod his head?
  What a pity, sir, that dogs can't talk!
He understands every word that's said —
  And he knows good milk from water-and-chalk.

The truth is, sir, now I reflect,
    I've been so sadly given to grog,
I wonder I've not lost the respect
    (Here's to you, sir!) even of my dog.
But he sticks by, through thick and thin;
    And this old coat, with its empty pockets,
And rags that smell of tobacco and gin,
    He'll follow while he has eyes in his sockets.

There isn't another creature living
    Would do it, and prove through every disaster
So fond, so faithful, and so forgiving,
    To such a miserable, thankless master.
No, sir! — see him wag his tail and grin;
    By George! it makes my old eyes water;
That is, there's something in this gin
    That chokes a fellow.   But no matter!

We'll have some music if you're willing,
    And Roger (hem! what a plague a cough is, sir!)
Shall march a little. — Start, you villain!
    Paws up! Eyes front! Salute your officer!
'Bout face! Attention! Take your rifle!
    (Some dogs have arms, you see.)   Now hold your
Cap while the gentlemen give a trifle,
    To aid a poor old patriot soldier.

March! Halt! Now show how the rebel shakes
    When he stands up to hear his sentence.
Now tell us how many drams it takes
    To honor a jolly new acquaintance.
Five yelps — that's five; he's mighty knowing!
    The night's before us, fill the glasses;
Quick, sir! I'm ill — my brain is going —
    Some brandy — thank you.   There! — it passes.

Why not reform?   That's easily said;
    But I've gone through such wretched treatment —
Sometimes forgetting the taste of bread,
    And scarce remembering what meat meant —
That my poor stomach's past reform;
    And there are times when, mad with thinking,
I'd sell out heaven for something warm
    To prop a horrible inward sinking.

Is there a way to forget to think?
    At your age, sir: home, fortune, friends,
A dear girl's love — but I took to drink;
    The same old story; you know how it ends.
If you could have seen these classic features —
    You needn't laugh, sir; they were not then
Such a burning libel on God's creatures:
    I was one of your handsome men!

If you had seen her, so fair and young,
    Whose head was happy on this breast;
If you could have heard the songs I sung
    When the wine went round, you wouldn't have guessed
That ever I, sir, should be straying
    From door to door, with fiddle and dog,
Ragged and penniless, and playing
    To you tonight for a glass of grog.

She's married since — a parson's wife:
    'Twas better for her that we should part;
Better the soberest, prosiest life
    Than a blasted home and a broken heart.
I have seen her?   Once: I was weak and spent
    On the dusty road; a carriage stopped;
But she little dreamed, as on she went,
    Who kissed the coin that her fingers dropped.

You've set me talking, sir; I'm sorry:
    It makes me wild to think of the change.
What do you care for a beggar's story?
    Is it amusing?   You find it strange?
I had a mother so proud of me;
    'Twas well she died before. — Do you know
If the happy spirits in heaven can see
    The ruin and wretchedness here below?

Another glass, and strong, to deaden
    This pain; then Roger and I will start.
I wonder, has he such a lumpish, leaden,
    Aching thing in place of a heart?
He is sad sometimes, and would weep, if he could,
    No doubt remembering things that were:
A virtuous kennel, with plenty of food,
    And himself a sober, respectable cur.

I'm better now; that glass was warming. —
    You rascal! limber your lazy feet!
We must be fiddling and performing
    For supper and bed, or starve in the street. —
Not a very gay life to lead, you think?
    But soon we shall go where lodgings are free,
And the sleepers need neither victuals nor drink:
    The sooner, the better for Roger and me.

The Burial of Sir John Moore

CHARLES WOLFE

The double rhymes tend to quicken the movement of the rhythm, and thus help suggest the haste with which the soldiers had to bury their fallen hero. The alternating single rhymes strike upon the ear with a slow, tolling sound, like a funeral knell.

Not a drum was heard, not a funeral note,
  As his corpse to the rampart we hurried;
Not a soldier discharged his farewell shot
  O'er the grave where our hero we buried.

We buried him darkly at dead of night,
  The sods with our bayonets turning,
By the struggling moonbeam's misty light,
  And the lantern dimly burning.

No useless coffin enclosed his breast,
  Not in sheet nor in shroud we wound him;
But he lay like a warrior taking his rest,
  With his martial cloak around him.

Few and short were the prayers we said,
  And we spoke not a word of sorrow;
But we steadfastly gazed on the face that was dead,
  And we bitterly thought of the morrow.

We thought, as we hollowed his narrow bed,
  And smoothed down his lonely pillow,
That the foe and the stranger would tread o'er his head,
  And we far away on the billow!

Lightly they'll talk of the spirit that's gone,
  And o'er his cold ashes upbraid him;
But little he'll reck, if they let him sleep on
  In the grave where a Briton has laid him.

But half of our heavy task was done
  When the clock struck the hour for retiring;
And we heard the distant and random gun
  That the foe was sullenly firing.

Slowly and sadly we laid him down,
  From the field of his fame fresh and gory;
We carved not a line, and we raised not a stone —
  But we left him alone with his glory!

Requiem

ROBERT LOUIS STEVENSON

*These are the lines which the poet wrote for his own grave.
The word "requiem" comes from a Latin word meaning rest.*

Under the wide and starry sky
Dig the grave and let me lie;
Glad did I live and gladly die,
  And I laid me down with a will.

This be the verse you grave for me:
*Here he lies where he longed to be;
Home is the sailor, home from the sea,
  And the hunter home from the hill.*

To Night

Percy Bysshe Shelley

*The rhymes wind in and out of these stanzas like strains of soft,
beautiful music, heard in a dream.*

Swiftly walk o'er the western wave,
     Spirit of Night!
Out of the misty eastern cave,
Where, all the long and lone daylight,
Thou wovest dreams of joy and fear,
Which make thee terrible and dear —
     Swift be thy flight!

Wrap thy form in a mantle gray,
     Star-inwrought!
Blind with thine hair the eyes of Day;
Kiss her until she be wearied out;
Then wander o'er city and sea and land,
Touching all with thine opiate wand —
     Come, long-sought!

When I arose and saw the dawn,
     I sighed for thee;
When light rode high, and the dew was gone,
And noon lay heavy on flower and tree,
And the weary Day turned to her rest,
Lingering like an unloved guest,
     I sighed for thee.

Thy brother Death came, and cried,
      "Wouldst thou me?"
Thy sweet child Sleep, the filmy-eyed,
Murmured like a noontide bee,
"Shall I nestle near thy side?
Wouldst thou me?" — And I replied,
      "No, not thee!"

Death will come when thou art dead,
      Soon, too soon —
Sleep will come when thou art fled;
Of neither would I ask the boon
I ask of thee, beloved Night —
Swift be thine approaching flight,
      Come soon, soon!

The Raven

Edgar Allan Poe

These lines waken harmonies of rhyme as musical as chords that vibrate from a golden harp.

Once upon a midnight dreary, while I pondered, weak
    and weary,
Over many a quaint and curious volume of forgotten lore —
While I nodded, nearly napping, suddenly there came a
    tapping,
As of someone gently rapping, rapping at my chamber
    door.
" 'Tis some visitor," I muttered, "tapping at my chamber
    door:
        Only this and nothing more."

Ah, distinctly I remember it was in the bleak December,
And each separate dying ember wrought its ghost upon the
    floor.
Eagerly I wished the morrow; — vainly I had sought to
    borrow
From my books surcease of sorrow — sorrow for the lost
    Lenore,
For the rare and radiant maiden whom the angels name
    Lenore:
        Nameless here for evermore.

And the silken sad uncertain rustling of each purple curtain
Thrilled me — filled me with fantastic terrors never felt
    before;

So that now, to still the beating of my heart, I stood repeat·
   ing,
" 'Tis some visitor entreating entrance at my chamber door,
Some late visitor entreating entrance at my chamber door:
          This it is and nothing more."

Presently my soul grew stronger; hesitating then no longer,
"Sir," said I, "or Madam, truly your forgiveness I implore;
But the fact is I was napping, and so gently you came
   rapping,
And so faintly you came tapping, tapping at my chamber
   door,
That I scarce was sure I heard you" — here I opened wide
   the door: —
          Darkness there and nothing more.

Deep into that darkness peering, long I stood there wonder-
   ing, fearing,
Doubting, dreaming dreams no mortal ever dared to dream
   before;
But the silence was unbroken, and the stillness gave no
   token,
And the only word there spoken was the whispered word,
   "Lenore?"
This I whispered, and an echo murmured back the word,
   "Lenore":
          Merely this and nothing more.

Back into the chamber turning, all my soul within me
   burning,
Soon again I heard a tapping somewhat louder than before.
"Surely," said I, "surely that is something at my window
   lattice;

Let me see, then, what thereat is, and this mystery explore;
Let my heart be still a moment and this mystery explore:
          'Tis the wind and nothing more."

Open here I flung the shutter, when, with many a flirt and
          flutter,
In there stepped a stately Raven of the saintly days of yore.
Not the least obeisance made he; not a minute stopped or
          stayed he;
But with mien of lord or lady, perched above my chamber
          door,
Perched upon a bust of Pallas just above my chamber door:
          Perched, and sat, and nothing more.

Then this ebony bird beguiling my sad fancy into smiling
By the grave and stern decorum of the countenance it
          wore, —
"Though thy crest be shorn and shaven, thou," I said, "art
          sure no craven,
Ghastly grim and ancient Raven wandering from the
          Nightly shore:
Tell me what thy lordly name is on the Night's Plutonian
          shore!"
          Quoth the Raven, "Nevermore."

Much I marveled this ungainly fowl to hear discourse so
          plainly,
Though its answer little meaning — little relevancy bore;
For we cannot help agreeing that no living human being
Ever yet was blessed with seeing bird above his chamber
          door,
Bird or beast upon the sculptured bust above his chamber
          door,
          With such name as "Nevermore."

But the Raven, sitting lonely on the placid bust, spoke only
That one word, as if his soul in that one word he did
outpour.
Nothing further then he uttered, not a feather then he
fluttered,
Till I scarcely more than muttered, — "Other friends have
flown before;
On the morrow he will leave me, as my Hopes have flown
before."
Then the bird said, "Nevermore."

Startled at the stillness broken by reply so aptly spoken,
"Doubtless," said I, "what it utters is its only stock and
store,
Caught from some unhappy master whom unmerciful
Disaster
Followed fast and followed faster till his songs one burden
bore:
Till the dirges of his Hope that melancholy burden bore
Of 'Never — nevermore.' "

But the Raven still beguiling all my fancy into smiling,
Straight I wheeled a cushioned seat in front of bird and bust
and door;
Then, upon the velvet sinking, I betook myself to linking
Fancy unto fancy, thinking what this ominous bird of yore,
What this grim, ungainly, ghastly, gaunt, and ominous
bird of yore
Meant in croaking "Nevermore."

This I sat engaged in guessing, but no syllable expressing
To the fowl whose fiery eyes now burned into my bosom's
core;
This and more I sat divining, with my head at ease reclining

On the cushion's velvet lining that the lamplight gloated
o'er,
But whose velvet violet lining with the lamplight gloating
o'er

She shall press, ah, nevermore!

Then, methought, the air grew denser, perfumed from an
unseen censer
Swung by seraphim whose footfalls tinkled on the tufted
floor.
"Wretch," I cried, "thy God hath lent thee — by these
angels he hath sent thee
Respite — respite and nepenthe from thy memories of
Lenore!
Quaff, oh quaff this kind nepenthe, and forget this lost
Lenore!"

Quoth the Raven, "Nevermore."

"Prophet!" said I, "thing of evil! — prophet still, if bird or
devil!
Whether Tempter sent, or whether tempest tossed thee here
ashore,
Desolate yet all undaunted, on this desert land enchanted —
On this home by Horror haunted — tell me truly, I
implore:
Is there — *is* there balm in Gilead? — tell me —tell me,
I implore!"

Quoth the Raven, "Nevermore."

"Prophet!" said I, "thing of evil — prophet still, if bird or
devil!
By that Heaven that bends above us, by that God we both
adore,
Tell this soul with sorrow laden if, within the distant Aidenn,

It shall clasp a sainted maiden whom the angels name
    Lenore:
Clasp a rare and radiant maiden whom the angels name
    Lenore!''
        Quoth the Raven, "Nevermore."

"Be that word our sign of parting, bird or fiend!" I
    shrieked, upstarting:
"Get thee back into the tempest and the Night's Plutonian
    shore!
Leave no black plume as a token of that lie thy soul hath
    spoken!
Leave my loneliness unbroken! quit the bust above my
    door!
Take thy beak from out my heart, and take thy form from
    off my door!"
        Quoth the Raven, "Nevermore."

And the Raven, never flitting, still is sitting, still is sitting
On the pallid bust of Pallas just above my chamber door;
And his eyes have all the seeming of a demon's that is
    dreaming,
And the lamplight o'er him streaming throws his shadow on
    the floor;
And my soul from out that shadow that lies floating on the
    floor
        Shall be lifted — nevermore!

Seaweed

HENRY WADSWORTH LONGFELLOW

*Somewhat of the sound and movement of the toiling sea is suggested by
these polysyllabic rhymes and the lines that shift in length from long to short.*

When descends on the Atlantic
  The gigantic
Storm-wind of the equinox,
Landward in his wrath he scourges
  The toiling surges,
Laden with seaweed from the rocks:

From Bermuda's reefs; from edges
  Of sunken ledges,
In some far-off, bright Azore;
From Bahama, and the dashing,
  Silver-flashing
Surges of San Salvador;

From the tumbling surf, that buries
  The Orkneyan skerries,
Answering the hoarse Hebrides;
And from wrecks of ships, and drifting
  Spars, uplifting
On the desolate, rainy seas; —

Ever drifting, drifting, drifting
  On the shifting
Currents of the restless main;
Till in sheltered coves and reaches
  Of sandy beaches,
All have found repose again.

So when storms of wild emotion
    Strike the ocean
Of the poet's soul, ere long
From each cave and rocky fastness,
    In its vastness,
Floats some fragment of a song:

Ever drifting, drifting, drifting
    On the shifting
Currents of the restless heart;
Till at length in books recorded,
    They, like hoarded
Household words, no more depart.

The Eagle

ALFRED, LORD TENNYSON

The rhymes seem to help speed the eagle's flight.

He clasps the crag with crooked hands;
Close to the sun in lonely lands,
Ringed with the azure world, he stands.

The wrinkled sea beneath him crawls;
He watches from his mountain walls,
And like a thunderbolt he falls.

Play

CHARLES STUART CALVERLEY

*These rhymes must be on a holiday, so jocund are they!   Indeed, they grow
so irresponsible that they care not a whit for consequences.*

Play, play, while yet it is day:
While yet the sweet sunlight is warm on the brae!
Hark to the lark singing lay upon lay,
While the brown squirrel eats nuts on the spray,
And in the apple leaves chatters the jay;
Play, play, even as they!
What though the cowslips ye pluck will decay,
What though the grass will be presently hay?
What though the noise that ye make should dismay
Old Mrs. Clutterbuck over the way?
Play, play, for your locks will grow gray;
Even the marbles ye sport with are clay.

Play, aye in the crowded highway:
Was it not made for you?   Yea, my lad, yea!
True that the babes you were bid to convey
Home may fall out or be stolen or stray;
True that the tip-cat you toss about may
Strike an old gentleman, cause him to sway,
Stumble, and p'raps be run o'er by a dray:
Still, why delay?   Play, my son, play!
Barclay and Perkins, not you, have to pay.

Play, play, your sonatas in A,
Heedless of what your next neighbor may say!
Dance and be gay as a faun or a fay,

Sing like the lad in the boat on the bay;
Sing, play — if your neighbors inveigh
Feebly against you, they're lunatics, eh?
Bang, twang, clatter and clang,
Strum, thrum, upon fiddle and drum;
Neigh, bray, simply obey
All your sweet impulses, stop not or stay!
Rattle the "bones," hit a tin-bottomed tray
Hard with the fire shovel, hammer away!
Is not your neighbor your natural prey?
Should he confound you, it's only in play.

Cradle Song

JOSIAH GILBERT HOLLAND

What is the little one thinking about?
Very wonderful things, no doubt:
    Unwritten history!
    Unfathomed mystery!
Yet he chuckles and crows, and nods and winks,
As if his head were as full of kinks
And curious riddles as any sphinx!
    Warped by colic, and wet by tears,
    Punctured by pins, and tortured by fears,
    Our little nephew will lose two years;
        And he'll never know
        Where the summers go:
He need not laugh, for he'll find it so!

The Lord Chancellor's Song

W. S. GILBERT

*Of course a Lord Chancellor is always an exceedingly proper and dignified
fellow. You can tell that by the length of the lines. . . . What, you
don't believe it?*

When you're lying awake with a dismal headache, and
    repose is tabooed by anxiety,
I conceive you may use any language you choose to indulge
    in, without impropriety;
For your brain is on fire — the bedclothes conspire of usual
    slumber to plunder you:
First your counterpane goes and uncovers your toes, and
    your sheet slips demurely from under you;
Then the blanketing tickles — you feel like mixed pickles —
    so terribly sharp is the pricking,
And you're hot, and you're cross, and you tumble and toss
    till there's nothing 'twixt you and the ticking.
Then the bed clothes all creep to the ground in a heap, and
    you pick 'em all up in a tangle;
Next your pillow resigns and politely declines to remain at
    its usual angle!
Well, you get some repose in the form of a doze, with hot
    eyeballs and head ever aching,
But your slumbering teems with such horrible dreams that
    you'd very much better be waking;
For you dream you are crossing the Channel, and tossing
    about in a steamer from Harwich —
Which is something between a large bathing-machine and a
    very small second-class carriage —

[141]

You're a regular wreck, with a crick in your neck, and nc
    wonder you snore, for your head's on the floor, and
    you've needles and pins from your soles to your shins,
    and your flesh is a-creep, for your left leg's asleep,
    and you've cramp in your toes, and a fly on your nose,
    and some fluff in your lung, and a feverish tongue,
    and a thirst that's intense, and a general sense that
    you haven't been sleeping in clover;
But the darkness has passed, and it's daylight at last, and
    the night has been long — ditto ditto my song —
    and thank goodness they're both of them over!

Jenny Kissed Me

Leigh Hunt

Jenny kissed me when we met,
    Jumping from the chair she sat in;
Time, you thief, who love to get
    Sweets into your list, put that in!
Say I'm weary say I'm sad;
    Say that health and wealth have missed me;
Say I'm growing old, but add,
        Jenny kissed me!

The Modern Major-General

W. S. GILBERT

*He may not know much about military matters, but there is no doubt of
his ability to make polysyllabic rhymes!*

I am the very model of a modern Major-General.
I've information vegetable, animal, and mineral;
I know the kings of England, and I quote the fights
      historical,
From Marathon to Waterloo, in order categorical;
I'm very well acquainted too with matters mathematical,
I understand equations, both the simple and quadratical,
About binomial theorem I'm teeming with a lot o' news,
With many cheerful facts about the square of the hypote-
      nuse.

I'm very good at integral and differential calculus,
I know the scientific names of beings animalculous,
In short, in matters vegetable, animal, and mineral,
I am the very model of a modern Major-General.

THE · MOVASTAR · WAS · A · BETTER · BOAT
BUT · THE · BELLE · SHE · WOULDN'T · BE · PASSED

VII: PATTERN AND STANZA

"Pattern in poetry?" says someone. Many things have pattern — dresses, oak leaves, snowflakes. Even people are made according to a pattern — two arms, two legs, one head. But what has pattern to do with poetry?

Pattern is design. It means orderly arrangement. It means symmetry or balance of one part with another. The two sides of the face are symmetrical, eye matching eye, eyebrow matching eyebrow, and cheek, cheek. The petals of a daisy grow in a symmetric pattern around a center. Indeed, wherever one looks, there are examples of symmetry and pattern: the two straight rows of buttons on a coat, the starry points of a snowflake, the orderly array of red and black squares on a checkerboard.

People are so made that they enjoy symmetry. They like the parts of a thing to be proportionate. A tree with all the branches chopped off on one side looks unbalanced. It is this same lop-sidedness that makes a person with the mumps look so funny.

Because pattern gives pleasure, the poet strives for symmetry. He uses a definite rhythmic measure. He takes care that lines shall be balanced in length. Sometimes he alternates long lines and short ones; sometimes he makes them all alike; sometimes he counterpoises, or balances, two short lines against a long one. But he always has some plan of arrangement.

Another aid to symmetry is rhyme. Lines which match in length are often matched in sound by rhyming words.

Besides rhythm, balance in length of line, and rhyme, a fourth element in poetic pattern is stanza. The stanza corresponds to the paragraph in prose.

There are many kinds of stanzas, ranging from the simple couplet (a two-line stanza) to long and elaborate forms. The poet may contrive a new stanza form to fit his thought and mood, or he may use a form with which he is already familiar.

Some stanza forms are so frequently used that they have been given names. The best known of these is the ballad stanza. It is the stanza in which many of the old ballads for singing were composed. The ballad stanza consists of four lines in iambic meter. The first and third lines each contain four measures; the second and fourth lines, three measures. The two short lines must rhyme; the other two lines may rhyme.

> The pines were dark on Ramoth hill,
> Their song was soft and low;
> The blossoms in the sweet May wind
> Were falling like the snow.

The sonnet, one of the most difficult of stanza forms to write, is one of the most beautiful and dignified. It always consists of fourteen lines of iambic pentameter and follows a scheme of interwoven rhymes. On page 167 may be found one of the finest sonnets in the English language.

The Ballad of the Oysterman

OLIVER WENDELL HOLMES

Long lines are eminently suitable for so mournful a ballad, but something (is it only the matter-of-fact jingle of the rhyming couplets?) keeps you from becoming too melancholy as you read.

It was a tall young oysterman lived by the river-side,
His shop was just upon the bank, his boat was on the tide;
The daughter of a fisherman, that was so straight and slim,
Lived over on the other bank, right opposite to him.

It was the pensive oysterman that saw a lovely maid,
Upon a moonlight evening, a-sitting in the shade;
He saw her wave her handkerchief, as much as if to say,
"I'm wide awake, young oysterman, and all the folks away."

Then up arose the oysterman, and to himself said he,
"I guess I'll leave the skiff at home, for fear that folks should
        see;
I read it in the story book, that, for to kiss his dear,
Leander swam the Hellespont — and I will swim this here."

And he has leaped into the waves, and crossed the shining
        stream,
And he has clambered up the bank, all in the moonlight
        gleam;
Oh, there were kisses sweet as dew, and words as soft as
        rain —
But they have heard her father's step, and in he leaps
        again!

Out spoke the ancient fisherman: "Oh, what was that, my
        daughter?"
"'Twas nothing but a pebble, sir, I threw into the water."
"And what is that, pray tell me, love, that paddles off so
        fast?"
"It's nothing but a porpoise, sir, that's been a-swimming
        past."

Out spoke the ancient fisherman: "Now bring me my har-
        poon!
I'll get into my fishing boat, and fix the fellow soon."
Down fell that pretty innocent, as falls a snow-white lamb,
Her hair drooped round her pallid cheeks, like seaweed on a
        clam.

Alas for those two loving ones! she waked not from her
        swound,
And he was taken with the cramp, and in the waves was
        drowned;
But Fate has metamorphosed them, in pity of their woe,
And now they keep an oyster shop for mermaids down below.

Jim Bludso of the Prairie Belle

JOHN HAY

The measured rhythm, the rhyme, and the stanza pattern lend something of beauty to the homely speech of the old riverman. So it was with Jim Bludso himself — a mixture of roughness and nobility.

Wall, no! I can't tell whar he lives,
  Becase he don't live, you see;
Leastways, he's got out of the habit
  Of livin' like you and me.
Whar have you been for the last three year
  That you haven't heard folks tell
How Jimmy Bludso passed in his checks
  The night of the Prairie Belle?

He weren't no saint, — them engineers
  Is all pretty much alike, —
One wife in Natchez-under-the-Hill
  And another one here, in Pike;
A keerless man in his talk was Jim,
  And an awkward hand in a row,
But he never flunked, and he never lied —
  I reckon he never knowed how.

And this was all the religion he had —
  To treat his engine well;
Never be passed on the river;
  To mind the pilot's bell;
And if ever the Prairie Belle took fire,
  A thousand times he swore
He'd hold her nozzle agin the bank
  Till the last soul got ashore.

[149]

All boats has their day on the Mississip,
  And her day come at last, —
The Movastar was a better boat,
  But the Belle she *wouldn't* be passed.
And so she came tearin' along that night,
  The oldest craft on the line,
With a nigger squat on her safety valve,
  And her furnace crammed, rosin and pine.

The fire bust out as she clared the bar,
  And burnt a hole in the night,
And quick as a flash she turned, and made
  For that willer-bank on the right.
There was runnin' and cursin', but Jim yelled out,
  Over the infernal roar,
"I'll hold her nozzle agin the bank
  Till the last galoot's ashore."

Through the hot, black breath of the burnin' boat
  Jim Bludso's voice was heard,
And they all had trust in his cussedness,
  And knowed he would keep his word.
And, sure's you're born, they all got off
  Afore the smokestacks fell, —
And Bludso's ghost went up alone
  In the smoke of the Prairie Belle.

He weren't no saint, — but at jedgment
  I'd run my chance with Jim,
'Longside of some pious gentlemen
  That wouldn't shook hands with him.
He seen his duty, a dead-sure thing, —
  And went for it thar and then;
And Christ ain't a-going to be too hard
  On a man that died for men.

Limericks

COSMO MONKHOUSE

Although the limerick is written only for fun, it follows a strict pattern. Can you work out the pattern?

There was a young lady from Niger,
Who smiled as she rode on a tiger.
They came back from the ride
With the lady inside,
And the smile on the face of the tiger.

The poor benighted Hindoo,
He does the best he kindo;
He sticks to caste
From first to last;
For pants he makes his skindo.

An Eggstravagance

OLIVER WENDELL HOLMES

The Reverend Henry Ward Beecher
Called a hen a most elegant creature.
The hen, pleased with that,
Laid an egg in his hat —
And thus did the hen reward Beecher!

[151]

The Valley That God Forgot

H. H. KNIBBS

This story of the thirst-driven prospector is set in a pattern which pleases the eye as well as the ear. The dignity of the poetic pattern suggests the earnestness with which the strange story is told.

Out in the desert spaces, edged by a hazy blue,
Davison sought the faces of the long-lost friends he knew:
      They were there, in the distance dreaming
      Their dreams that were worn and old;
      They were there, to his frenzied seeming,
      Still burrowing down for gold.

Davison's face was leather; his mouth was a swollen blot,
His mind was a floating feather, in the Valley That God
      Forgot;
      Wild as a dog gone loco,
      Or sullen or meek, by turns,
      He mumbled a "Poco! Poco!"
      And whispered of pools and ferns.

Gold! Why his, for the finding! But water was never
      found,
Save in deep caverns winding miles through the under-
      ground:
      Cool, far, shadowy places
      Edged by the mirrored trees,
      When — Davison saw the faces!
      And fear let loose his knees.

There was Shorty who owed him money, and Billing who
          bossed the crowd;
And Steve whom the boys called "Sunny," and Collins
          who talked so loud:
          Miguel with the handsome daughter,
          And the rustler, Ed McCray;
          Five — and they begged for water,
          And offered him gold, in pay.

Gold? It was never cheaper. And Davison shook his
          head:
"The price of a drink is steeper out here than in town," he
          said.
          He laughed as they mouthed and muttered
          Through lips that were cracked and dried;
          The pulse in his eardrum fluttered:
          "I'm through with the game!" he cried.

"I'm through!"   And he knelt and fumbled the cap of his
          dry canteen;
Then, rising, he swayed and stumbled into a black ravine:
          His ghostly comrades followed,
          For Davison's end was near,
          And a shallow grave they hollowed,
          When up from it, cool and clear,

Bubbled the water — hidden a pick-stroke beneath the
          sand;
Davison, phantom-ridden, scooped with a shaking hand . . .
          Davison swears they made it,
          The Well where we drank today.
          Davison's game? He played it
          And won — so the town-folk say:

Called it, The Morning-Glory — near those abandoned
　　　　　stamps,
And Davison's crazy story was told in a hundred camps:
　　　　Time and the times have tamed it,
　　　　His yarn — and this desert spot,
　　　　But I'm strong for the man who named it,
　　　　The Valley That God Forgot.

Three Things to Remember

WILLIAM BLAKE

The poet's wisdom is compacted into couplets as brief as proverbs.

A Robin Redbreast in a cage
Puts all Heaven in a rage.

A skylark wounded on the wing
Doth make a cherub cease to sing.

He who shall hurt the little wren
Shall never be beloved by men.

The Old Familiar Faces

CHARLES LAMB

The recurrent phrase in the last line of the unrhymed triplets suggests how the poet's thoughts keep returning to the days of his childhood.

I have had playmates, I have had companions,
In my days of childhood, in my joyful schooldays —
All, all are gone, the old familiar faces.

I have been laughing, I have been carousing,
Drinking late, sitting late, with my bosom cronies —
All, all are gone, the old familiar faces.

I loved a Love once, fairest among women:
Closed are her doors on me, I must not see her —
All, all are gone, the old familiar faces.

I have a friend, a kinder friend has no man:
Like an ingrate, I left my friend abruptly;
Left him, to muse on the old familiar faces.

Ghost-like I paced round the haunts of my childhood,
Earth seemed a desert I was bound to traverse,
Seeking to find the old familiar faces.

Friend of my bosom, thou more than a brother,
Why wert thou not born in my father's dwelling?
So might we talk of the old familiar faces —

How some they have died, and some they have left me,
And some are taken from me; all are departed —
All, all are gone, the old familiar faces.

Little Boy Blue

EUGENE FIELD

These stanzas seem to have something of the stanchness and uprightness of the faithful little toy soldier.

The little toy dog is covered with dust,
But sturdy and stanch he stands;
And the little toy soldier is red with rust,
And his musket moulds in his hands.
Time was when the little toy dog was new,
And the soldier was passing fair;
And that was the time when our Little Boy Blue
Kissed them and put them there.

"Now, don't you go till I come," he said,
"And don't you make any noise!"
So, toddling off to his trundle-bed,
He dreamt of the pretty toys;
And as he was dreaming, an angel song
Awakened our Little Boy Blue —
Oh! the years are many, the years are long,
But the little toy friends are true!

Aye, faithful to Little Boy Blue they stand,
Each in the same old place —
Awaiting the touch of a little hand,
The smile of a little face;
And they wonder, as waiting the long years through
In the dust of that little chair,
What has become of our Little Boy Blue,
Since he kissed them and put them there.

My Playmate

John Greenleaf Whittier

*The ballad stanza may be used for telling almost any kind of incident,
humorous or exciting or, as in this poem, gently melancholy. You may
be interested in writing a ballad yourself. The stanza pattern is not difficult to follow.*

The pines were dark on Ramoth hill,
   Their song was soft and low;
The blossoms in the sweet May wind
   Were falling like the snow.

The blossoms drifted at our feet,
   The orchard birds sang clear;
The sweetest and the saddest day
   It seemed of all the year.

For, more to me than birds or flowers,
   My playmate left her home,
And took with her the laughing spring,
   The music and the bloom.

She kissed the lips of kith and kin,
   She laid her hand in mine:
What more could ask the bashful boy
   Who fed her father's kine?

She left us in the bloom of May:
   The constant years told o'er
The seasons with as sweet May morns,
   But she came back no more.

I walk, with noiseless feet, the round
  Of uneventful years;
Still o'er and o'er I sow the spring
  And reap the autumn ears.

She lives where all the golden year
  Her summer roses blow;
The dusky children of the sun
  Before her come and go.

There haply with her jeweled hands
  She smooths her silken gown —
No more the homespun lap wherein
  I shook the walnuts down.

The wild grapes wait us by the brook,
  The brown nuts on the hill,
And still the May-day flowers make sweet
  The woods of Follymill.

The lilies blossom in the pond,
  The bird builds in the tree,
The dark pines sing on Ramoth hill
  The slow song of the sea.

I wonder if she thinks of them,
  And how the old time seems —
If ever the pines of Ramoth wood
  Are sounding in her dreams!

I see her face, I hear her voice:
  Does she remember mine?
And what to her is now the boy
  Who fed her father's kine?

What cares she that the orioles build
　　For other eyes than ours —
That other hands with nuts are filled,
　　And other laps with flowers?

O playmate in the golden time!
　　Our mossy seat is green,
Its fringing violets blossom yet,
　　The old trees o'er it lean.

The winds so sweet with birch and fern
　　A sweeter memory blow;
And there in spring the veeries sing
　　The song of long ago.

And still the pines of Ramoth wood
　　Are moaning like the sea —
The moaning of the sea of change
　　Between myself and thee!

The Revenge

A Ballad of the Fleet, 1591

ALFRED, LORD TENNYSON

No wonder Queen Elizabeth's little navy defeated the mighty Spanish Armada, if all her men were as daring as these of whom the seaman tells. The stanza form here is irregular, varying with the action of the narrative. Notice how the rhymes quicken the movement of the verses.

I

At Florés in the Azores Sir Richard Grenville lay,
And a pinnace, like a fluttered bird, came flying from far
     away;
"Spanish ships of war at sea! we have sighted fifty-three!"
Then sware Lord Thomas Howard: "'Fore God I am no
     coward;
But I cannot meet them here, for my ships are out of gear,
And the half my men are sick.   I must fly, but follow quick.
We are six ships of the line; can we fight with fifty-three?"

II

Then spake Sir Richard Grenville: "I know you are no
     coward;
You fly them for a moment to fight with them again.
But I've ninety men and more that are lying sick ashore.
I should count myself the coward if I left them, my Lord
     Howard,
To these Inquisition dogs and the devildoms of Spain."

III

So Lord Howard passed away with five ships of war that
     day,
Till he melted like a cloud in the silent summer heaven;

But Sir Richard bore in hand all his sick men from the land
Very carefully and slow,
Men of Bideford in Devon,
And we laid them on the ballast down below;
For we brought them all aboard,
And they blessed him in their pain, that they were not left to
      Spain,
To the thumbscrew and the stake, for the glory of the Lord.

IV

He had only a hundred seamen to work the ship and to
      fight,
And he sailed away from Florés till the Spaniard came in
      sight,
With his huge sea-castles heaving upon the weather bow.
"Shall we fight or shall we fly?
Good Sir Richard, tell us now,
For to fight is but to die!
There'll be little of us left by the time this sun is set."
And Sir Richard said again: "We be all good English men.
Let us bang these dogs of Seville, the children of the devil,
For I never turned my back upon Don or devil yet."

V

Sir Richard spoke and he laughed, and we roared a hurrah,
      and so
The little Revenge ran on sheer into the heart of the foe,
With her hundred fighters on deck, and her ninety sick
      below;
For half of their fleet to the right and half to the left were
      seen,
And the little Revenge ran on through the long sea-lane
      between.

VI

Thousands of their soldiers looked down from their decks
and laughed,
Thousands of their seamen made mock at the mad little
craft
Running on and on, till delayed
By their mountain-like San Philip that, of fifteen hundred
tons,
And up-shadowing high above us with her yawning tiers of
guns,
Took the breath from our sails, and we stayed.

VII

And while now the great San Philip hung above us like a
cloud
Whence the thunderbolt will fall
Long and loud,
Four galleons drew away
From the Spanish fleet that day,
And two upon the larboard and two upon the starboard lay,
And the battle-thunder broke from them all.

VIII

But anon the great San Philip, she bethought herself and
went,
Having that within her womb that had left her ill content;
And the rest they came aboard us, and they fought us hand
to hand
For a dozen times they came with their pikes and musque-
teers,
And a dozen times we shook 'em off as a dog that shakes his
ears
When he leaps from the water to the land.

IX

And the sun went down, and the stars came out far over the
summer sea,
But never a moment ceased the fight of the one and the
fifty-three.
Ship after ship, the whole night long, their high-built galleons came,
Ship after ship, the whole night long, with her battle-
thunder and flame;
Ship after ship, the whole night long, drew back with her
dead and her shame.
For some were sunk and many were shattered, and so could
fight us no more —
God of battles, was ever a battle like this in the world
before?

X

For he said, "Fight on! fight on!"
Though his vessel was all but a wreck;
And it chanced that, when half of the short summer night
was gone,
With a grisly wound to be dressed he had left the deck,
But a bullet struck him that was dressing it suddenly dead,
And himself he was wounded again in the side and the head,
And he said, "Fight on! fight on!"

XI

And the night went down, and the sun smiled out far over
the summer sea,
And the Spanish fleet with broken sides lay round us all in a
ring;
But they dared not touch us again, for they feared that we
still could sting,
So they watched what the end would be.

And we had not fought them in vain,
But in perilous plight were we,
Seeing forty of our poor hundred were slain,
And half of the rest of us maimed for life
In the crash of the cannonades and the desperate strife;
And the sick men down in the hold were most of them stark
    and cold,
And the pikes were all broken or bent, and the powder was
    all of it spent;
And the masts and the rigging were lying over the side;
But Sir Richard cried in his English pride:
"We have fought such a fight for a day and a night
As may never be fought again!
We have won great glory, my men!
And a day less or more
At sea or ashore,
We die — does it matter when?
Sink me the ship, Master Gunner — sink her, split her in
    twain!
Fall into the hands of God, not into the hands of Spain!"

XII

And the gunner said, "Ay, ay," but the seamen made reply:
"We have children, we have wives,
And the Lord hath spared our lives.
We will make the Spaniard promise, if we yield, to let us go;
We shall live to fight again and to strike another blow."
And the lion there lay dying, and they yielded to the foe.

XIII

And the stately Spanish men to their flagship bore him then,
Where they laid him by the mast, old Sir Richard caught at
    last,

And they praised him to his face with their courtly foreign
      grace;
But he rose upon their decks, and he cried:
"I have fought for Queen and Faith like a gallant man and
      true;
I have only done my duty as a man is bound to do.
With a joyful spirit I, Sir Richard Grenville, die!"
And he fell upon their decks, and he died.

XIV

And they stared at the dead that had been so valiant and
      true,
And had holden the power and the glory of Spain so cheap
That he dared her with one little ship and his English few;
Was he devil or man? He was devil for aught they knew,
But they sank his body with honor down into the deep,
And they manned the Revenge with a swarthier, alien crew,
And away she sailed with her loss and longed for her own;
When a wind from the lands they had ruined awoke from
      sleep,
And the water began to heave and the weather to moan,
And or ever that evening ended a great gale blew,
And a wave like the wave that is raised by an earthquake
      grew,
Till it smote on their hulls and their sails and their masts
      and their flags,
And the whole sea plunged and fell on the shot-shattered
      navy of Spain,
And the little Revenge herself went down by the island crags
To be lost evermore in the main.

A Red, Red Rose

Robert Burns

Because the ballad stanza lends itself particularly well to singing, it is often used for songs.   This poem has been set to charming music.

O my Luve's like a red, red rose
    That's newly sprung in June;
O my Luve's like the melodie
    That's sweetly played in tune.

As fair art thou, my bonnie lass,
    So deep in luve am I;
And I will luve thee still, my dear,
    Till a' the seas gang dry.

Till a' the seas gang dry, my dear,
    And the rocks melt wi' the sun;
I will luve thee still, my dear,
    While the sands o' life shall run.

And fare thee weel, my only Luve,
    And fare thee weel a while!
And I will come again, my Luve,
    Though it were ten thousand mile.

On His Blindness

JOHN MILTON

The sonnet is a stately pattern, and the language of the blind poet has a grave and stately beauty.

When I consider how my light is spent,
Ere half my days in this dark world and wide,
And that one talent which is death to hide
Lodged with me useless, though my soul more bent
To serve therewith my Maker, and present
My true account, lest He returning chide;
"Doth God exact day labor, light denied?"
I fondly ask.   But Patience, to prevent
That murmur, soon replies: "God doth not need
Either man's work or his own gifts.   Who best
Bear his mild yoke, they serve him best.   His state
Is kingly; thousands at his bidding speed
And post o'er land and ocean without rest: —
They also serve who only stand and wait."

AND · DARK · IN · THE · DARK · OLD · INN · YARD · A · STABLE-WICKET · CREAKED
WHERE · TIM · THE · OSTLER · LISTENED · HIS · FACE · WAS · WHITE · AND · PEAKED

VIII:

CHANGE AND RECURRENCE

A November wind drives against door and windows. The little boy is tired of play with toy bear and drum. He is tired of standing, with small cold nose pressed tight against the glass, to watch the silver regiments of rain go slanting by.

"Tell me a story," he begs, "the story of the old woman and her pig."

What does it matter that he has heard it over and over? Again he is rapt away on the wings of recurring, familiar phrases.

> Stick, stick, beat dog.
> Dog won't bite pig,
> Pig won't get over the stile,
> And I shall not get home tonight.

After the pig jumps over the stile, there are other stories. Little Red Riding Hood reiterates her time-honored questions: "Grandmother, what makes your hands so big?" . . . "Grandmother, what makes your voice so deep?"

Goldilocks visits again the house of the Three Bears. . . . "She tasted the big bowl of porridge. It was too hot. She tasted the middle-sized bowl of porridge. It was too cold. She tasted the little bowl. It was just right. And she ate it all up."

How many children have been held spellbound by the familiar, repetitive phrases! You, yourself, when you were very young, were not deaf to their charm. They did not stale with repetition. Rather, part of their attraction lay in the fact that they were repeated — repeated so often that you learned to recognize them. And every time the story came around to certain parts, you felt a little private

[169]

thrill of ownership. You knew just what the next words would be.

She tried the Big Bear's bed. It was too hard. She tried the Middle-sized Bear's bed. It was too soft. She tried the Little Bear's bed.

The music maker knows the pleasure that comes of hearing the same sounds over and over. Therefore he repeats his musical phrases. Sometimes he repeats a whole passage in a chorus or a refrain.

The verse maker too knows the charm of recurrent sounds and phrases. Like the musician and the teller of stories for children, he makes use of repetition.

> Twenty years hence my eyes may grow,
> If not quite dim, yet rather so;
> Yet yours from others they shall know,
> Twenty years hence.

The recurrence of similar sounds and phrases helps to complete the verse pattern. They increase the musical effects also, somewhat as does the chorus of a song. And because they keep calling attention to the same idea, they intensify the meaning.

However, the story teller, the musician, and the poet must all beware of one danger. They must not repeat exactly what has gone before in exactly the same way. Repetition without change is monotonous. But repetition with change, even if the change is only in one note or word, or only in the position of the words, is delightful.

> By the flow of the inland river,
>   Whence the fleets of iron have fled,
> Where the blades of the grave-grass quiver,
>   Asleep are the ranks of the dead: —
>   Under the sod and the dew,
>   Waiting the Judgment Day;
>   Under the one, the Blue,
>   Under the other, the Gray.

These in the robings of glory,
   Those in the gloom of defeat,
All with the battle-blood gory,
   In the dusk of eternity meet: —
     Under the sod and the dew,
       Waiting the Judgment Day;
     Under the laurel, the Blue,
       Under the willow, the Gray.

Change and recurrence — the new and different added to the old and familiar — this satisfies the ear and the mind and the emotions.

The Wraggle Taggle Gipsies

Part of the quaint charm of ancient ballads is due to the recurrence of old-fashioned phrases and of syllables put in just for the sake of the rhythm and rhyme.

There were three gipsies a-come to my door,
And downstairs ran this a-lady, O!
One sang high, and another sang low,
And the other sang, Bonny, bonny Biscay, O!

Then she pulled off her silk-finished gown
And put on hose of leather, O!
The ragged, ragged rags about our door —
She's gone with the wraggle taggle gipsies, O!

It was late last night, when my lord came home,
Enquiring for his a-lady, O!
The servants said, on every hand:
"She's gone with the wraggle taggle gipsies, O!"

"O saddle to me my milk-white steed,
Go and fetch me my pony, O!
That I may ride and seek my bride,
Who is gone with the wraggle taggle gipsies, O!"

O he rode high and he rode low,
He rode through woods and copses too,
Until he came to an open field,
And there he espied his a-lady, O!

"What makes you leave your house and land?
What makes you leave your money, O?
What makes you leave your new-wedded lord,
To go with the wraggle taggle gipsies, O?"

"What care I for my house and my land?
What care I for my money, O?
What care I for my new-wedded lord?
I'm off with the wraggle taggle gipsies, O!"

"Last night you slept on a goose-feather bed,
With the sheet turned down so bravely, O!
And tonight you'll sleep in a cold open field,
Along with the wraggle taggle gipsies, O!"

"What care I for a goose-feather bed,
With the sheet turned down so bravely, O?
For tonight I shall sleep in a cold open field,
Along with the wraggle taggle gipsies, O!"

AN OLD BALLAD

Twenty Years Hence

WALTER SAVAGE LANDOR

Looking down the years, the poet sees himself grown dim of sight or perhaps laid to sleep in a silent grave. The repetition of "twenty years hence" seems to bring the time inescapably near.

Twenty years hence my eyes may grow,
If not quite dim, yet rather so;
Yet yours from others they shall know,
    Twenty years hence.

Twenty years hence, though it may hap
That I be called to take a nap
In a cool cell where thunder-clap
    Was never heard,

There breathe but o'er my arch of grass
A not too sadly sighed "Alas!"
And I shall catch, ere you can pass,
    That wingéd word.

Eileen Aroon

GERALD GRIFFIN

The poet plays upon the maiden's name as upon a harp string, for the music of its sound. The last stanza is one of the most beautiful in all Irish poetry.

When like the early rose,
      Eileen Aroon!
Beauty in childhood blows,
      Eileen Aroon!
When, like a diadem,
Buds blush around the stem,
Which is the fairest gem? —
      Eileen Aroon!

Is it the laughing eye,
      Eileen Aroon!
Is it the timid sigh,
      Eileen Aroon!
Is it the tender tone,
Soft as the stringed harp's moan?
O, it is truth alone, —
      Eileen Aroon!

When like the rising day,
      Eileen Aroon!
Love sends his early ray,
      Eileen Aroon!
What makes his dawning glow,
Changeless through joy or woe?
Only the constant know: —
      Eileen Aroon!

I know a valley fair,
        Eileen Aroon!
I knew a cottage there,
        Eileen Aroon!
Far in that valley's shade
I knew a gentle maid,
Flower of a hazel glade, —
        Eileen Aroon!

Who in the song so sweet?
        Eileen Aroon!
Who in the dance so fleet?
        Eileen Aroon!
Dear were her charms to me,
Dearer her laughter free,
Dearest her constancy, —
        Eileen Aroon!

Were she no longer true,
        Eileen Aroon!
What should her lover do?
        Eileen Aroon!
Fly with his broken chain
Far o'er the sounding main,
Never to love again, —
        Eileen Aroon!

Youth must with time decay,
        Eileen Aroon!
Beauty must fade away,
        Eileen Aroon!
Castles are sacked in war,
Chieftains are scattered far,
Truth is a fixéd star, —
        Eileen Aroon!

The House on the Hill

EDWIN ARLINGTON ROBINSON

*How the lonesomeness of the forsaken House is intensified by
telling of it over and over!*

They are all gone away,
    The House is shut and still,
There is nothing more to say.

Through broken walls and gray
    The winds blow bleak and shrill:
They are all gone away.

Nor is there one today
    To speak them good or ill:
There is nothing more to say.

Why is it then we stray,
    Around that sunken sill?
They are all gone away,

And our poor fancy-play
    For them is wasted skill:
There is nothing more to say.

There is ruin and decay
    In the House on the Hill:
They are all gone away,
There is nothing more to say.

The Highwayman

ALFRED NOYES

This swift, dramatic narrative owes much of its power to the repetition of phrases. They haunt the imagination with the magic of their sound and the vividness of their pictures.

PART ONE

The wind was a torrent of darkness among the gusty
    trees,
The moon was a ghostly galleon tossed upon cloudy seas,
The road was a ribbon of moonlight over the purple moor,
And the highwayman came riding —
        Riding — riding —
The highwayman came riding, up to the old inn door.

He'd a French cocked hat on his forehead, a bunch of lace at
    his chin,
A coat of the claret velvet, and breeches of brown doe-skin;
They fitted with never a wrinkle; his boots were up to the
    thigh!
And he rode with a jeweled twinkle,
        His pistol butts a-twinkle,
His rapier hilt a-twinkle, under the jeweled sky.

Over the cobbles he clattered and clashed in the dark inn
    yard;
And he tapped with his whip on the shutters, but all was
    locked and barred;

He whistled a tune to the window, and who should be
        waiting there
But the landlord's black-eyed daughter,
            Bess, the landlord's daughter,
Plaiting a dark red love knot into her long black hair.

And dark in the dark old inn yard a stable-wicket creaked
Where Tim the ostler listened; his face was white and
        peaked;
His eyes were hollows of madness, his hair like mouldy hay,
But he loved the landlord's daughter,
            The landlord's red-lipped daughter;
Dumb as a dog he listened, and he heard the robber say —

"One kiss, my bonny sweetheart; I'm after a prize tonight;
But I shall be back with the yellow gold before the morning
        light;
Yet, if they press me sharply, and harry me through the day,
Then look for me by moonlight,
            Watch for me by moonlight,
I'll come to thee by moonlight, though hell should bar the
        way."

He rose upright in the stirrups; he scarce could reach her
        hand,
But she loosened her hair i' the casement! His face burnt
        like a brand
As the black cascade of perfume came tumbling over his
        breast;
And he kissed its waves in the moonlight,
            (Oh, sweet black waves in the moonlight!)
Then he tugged at his rein in the moonlight, and galloped
        away to the West.

PART TWO

He did not come in the dawning; he did not come at
    noon;
And out o' the tawny sunset, before the rise o' the moon,
When the road was a gipsy's ribbon, looping the purple
    moor,
A redcoat troop came marching —
        Marching — marching —
King George's men came marching, up to the old inn door.

They said no word to the landlord; they drank his ale
    instead;
But they gagged his daughter and bound her to the foot of
    her narrow bed;
Two of them knelt at her casement, with muskets at their
    side!
There was death at every window;
        And hell at one dark window;
For Bess could see, through her casement, the road that *he*
    would ride.

They had tied her up to attention, with many a sniggering
    jest;
They had bound a musket beside her, with the barrel be-
    neath her breast!
"Now keep good watch!" and they kissed her.
She heard the dead man say:
Look for me by moonlight;
        Watch for me by moonlight;
I'll come to thee by moonlight, though hell should bar the way!

She twisted her hands behind her; but all the knots held
    good!
She writhed her hands till her fingers were wet with sweat
    or blood!
They stretched and strained in the darkness, and the hours
    crawled by like years,
Till, now, on the stroke of midnight,
        Cold on the stroke of midnight,
The tip of one finger touched it!   The trigger at least was
    hers!

The tip of one finger touched it; she strove no more for the
    rest!
Up, she stood up to attention, with the barrel beneath her
    breast.
She would not risk their hearing; she would not strive
    again;
For the road lay bare in the moonlight;
        Blank and bare in the moonlight;
And the blood of her veins in the moonlight throbbed to her
    love's refrain.

Tlot-tlot; tlot-tlot!   Had they heard it?   The horse-hoofs
    ringing clear;
Tlot-tlot, tlot-tlot, in the distance!   Were they deaf that they
    did not hear?
Down the ribbon of moonlight, over the brow of the hill,
The highwayman came riding,
        Riding, riding!
The redcoats looked to their priming!   She stood up,
    straight and still!

Tlot-tlot, in the frosty silence!   *Tlot-tlot,* in the echoing
      night!
Nearer he came and nearer!   Her face was like a light!
Her eyes grew wide for a moment; she drew one last deep
      breath;
Then her finger moved in the moonlight,
            Her musket shattered the moonlight,
Shattered her breast in the moonlight and warned him —
      with her death.

He turned; he spurred to the West; he did not know who
      stood
Bowed, with her head o'er the musket, drenched with her
      own red blood!
Not till the dawn he heard it, and his face grew gray to hear
How Bess, the landlord's daughter,
            The landlord's black-eyed daughter,
Had watched for her love in the moonlight, and died in the
      darkness there.

Back he spurred like a madman, shrieking a curse to the sky,
With the white road smoking behind him, and his rapier
      brandished high!
Blood-red were his spurs in the golden noon; wine-red was
      his velvet coat,
When they shot him down on the highway,
            Down like a dog on the highway,
And he lay in his blood on the highway, with the bunch of
      lace at his throat.

    .   .   .   .

And still of a winter's night, they say, when the wind is in the trees,
When the moon is a ghostly galleon tossed upon cloudy seas,
When the road is a ribbon of moonlight over the purple moor,
A highwayman comes riding —
              Riding — riding —
A highwayman comes riding, up to the old inn door.

Over the cobbles he clatters and clangs in the dark inn yard;
And he taps with his whip on the shutters, but all is locked and
           barred;
He whistles a tune to the window, and who should be waiting there
But the landlord's black-eyed daughter,
              Bess, the landlord's daughter,
Plaiting a dark red love knot into her long black hair.

I've Got a Dog

ETHEL KELLEY

"I've got a dog!" The owner is so happy and proud that he keeps repeating the important fact.

I've got a dog.   The other boys
Have quantities of tools and toys,
And heaps of things that I ain't seen
    (Ain't saw, I mean).
They've oars and clubs and golfin' sticks; —
I know a feller that has six,
    And gee! you ought to see him drive!
    But I've
        Got a dog!

I've got a dog.   His name is Pete.
    The other children on our street
Have lots of things that I ain't got
    (I mean, have not).
I know a boy that's got a gun —
I don't see why they have such fun
    Playing with things that ain't alive;
    But I've
        Got a dog!

I've got a dog, and so, you see,
    The boys all want to play with me;
They think he's such a cunnin' brute
    (I mean, so cute).

That's why they leave their toys and games,
And run to us, and shout our names,
    Whenever me and Pete arrive;
    For I've
        Got a dog!

Hie Away

SIR WALTER SCOTT

The invitation would not be half so alluring if it were not repeated.

Hie away, hie away,
Over bank and over brae,
Where the copsewood is the greenest,
Where the fountains glisten sheenest,
Where the lady-fern grows strongest,
Where the morning dew lies longest,
Where the black-cock sweetest sips it,
Where the fairy latest trips it:
Hie to haunts right seldom seen,
Lovely, lonesome, cool, and green,
Over bank and over brae,
Hie away, hie away.

A Song of Trust

Poetry in the Old Testament is built upon parallelism; that is, upon the repetition of the same idea in different words. The effect is one of strength and grandeur. This is the One Hundred Twenty-first Psalm

I will lift up mine eyes unto the hills,
From whence cometh my help.
My help cometh from the Lord,
Which made heaven and earth.
He will not suffer thy foot to be moved:
He that keepeth thee will not slumber.
Behold, he that keepeth Israel shall neither slumber nor
    sleep.
The Lord is thy keeper:
The Lord is thy shade upon thy right hand.
The sun shall not smite thee by day, nor the moon by night.
The Lord shall preserve thee from all evil:
He shall preserve thy soul.
The Lord shall preserve thy going out and thy coming in
    from this time forth, and even for evermore.

A SONG OF DAVID

The Blue and the Gray

FRANCIS MILES FINCH

The refrain recurs like a phrase in a requiem sung for the repose of the dead. This poem is said to have done more than any other one thing to heal the breach between North and South after the Civil War.

By the flow of the inland river,
  Whence the fleets of iron have fled,
Where the blades of the grave-grass quiver,
  Asleep are the ranks of the dead: —
    Under the sod and the dew,
      Waiting the Judgment Day;
    Under the one, the Blue,
      Under the other, the Gray.

These in the robings of glory,
  Those in the gloom of defeat,
All with the battle-blood gory,
  In the dusk of eternity meet: —
    Under the sod and the dew,
      Waiting the Judgment Day;
    Under the laurel, the Blue,
      Under the willow, the Gray.

From the silence of sorrowful hours
  The desolate mourners go,
Lovingly laden with flowers,
  Alike for the friend and the foe: —
    Under the sod and the dew,
      Waiting the Judgment Day;
    Under the roses, the Blue,
      Under the lilies, the Gray.

So with an equal splendor,
    The morning sun-rays fall,
With a touch impartially tender,
    On the blossoms blooming for all: —
        Under the sod and the dew,
            Waiting the Judgment Day;
        Broidered with gold, the Blue,
            Mellowed with gold, the Gray.

So when the summer calleth
    On forest and field of grain,
With an equal murmur falleth
    The cooling drip of the rain: —
        Under the sod and the dew,
            Waiting the Judgment Day;
        Wet with the rain, the Blue,
            Wet with the rain, the Gray.

Sadly but not with upbraiding,
    The generous deed was done;
In the storms of the years that are fading
    No braver battle was won: —
        Under the sod and the dew,
            Waiting the Judgment Day;
        Under the blossoms, the Blue,
            Under the garlands, the Gray.

No more shall the war-cry sever,
    Or the winding rivers be red;
They banish our anger forever,
    When they laurel the graves of our dead: —
        Under the sod and the dew,
            Waiting the Judgment Day;
        Love and tears for the Blue,
            Tears and love for the Gray.

I Remember

THOMAS HOOD

Try reading the poem with only one "I remember." Do you like it as well?

I remember, I remember,
The house where I was born,
The little window where the sun
Came peeping in at morn;
He never came a wink too soon,
Nor brought too long a day;
But now I often wish the night
Had borne my breath away.

I remember, I remember,
The roses, red and white,
The violets, and the lily-cups —
Those flowers made of light!
The lilacs where the robin built,
And where my brother set
The laburnum on his birthday —
The tree is living yet!

I remember, I remember,
Where I used to swing,
And thought the air must rush as fresh
To swallows on the wing;
My spirit flew in feathers then,
That is so heavy now,
And summer pools could hardly cool
The fever on my brow!

I remember, I remember,
The fir trees dark and high;
I used to think their slender tops
Were close against the sky:
It was a childish ignorance,
But now 'tis little joy
To know I'm farther off from heaven
Than when I was a boy.

Bonny George Campbell

Just why the repetition of a stanza should make the memory of the young clansman more haunting, it would be difficult to say.

Saddled and bridled
   And booted rade he;
Toom hame cam the saddle
   But never cam he.

Down cam his auld mither,
   Greetin' fu' sair,
And down cam his bonny bride
   Wringin' her hair.

Saddled and bridled
   And booted rade he;
Toom hame cam the saddle,
   But never cam he.

                              AN OLD BALLAD

The unfamiliar words here are Scotch terms. *Greetin' fu'
sair* means weeping or grieving very sadly.

Ballad

CHARLES STUART CALVERLEY

The rhymester is in mischievous mood, poking fun at venerable English ballads!

PART ONE

The auld wife sat at her ivied door,
   (*Butter and eggs and a pound of cheese*)
A thing she had frequently done before;
   And her spectacles lay on her aproned knees.

The piper he piped on the hilltop high,
   (*Butter and eggs and a pound of cheese*)
Till the cow said, "I die," and the goose asked, "Why?"
   And the dog said nothing, but searched for fleas.

The farmer he strode through the square farmyard;
   (*Butter and eggs and a pound of cheese*)
His last brew of ale was a trifle hard,
   The connection of which with the plot one sees.

The farmer's daughter hath frank blue eyes;
   (*Butter and eggs and a pound of cheese*)
She hears the rooks caw in the windy skies,
   As she sits at her lattice and shells her peas.

The farmer's daughter hath ripe red lips;
   (*Butter and eggs and a pound of cheese*)
If you try to approach her, away she skips
   Over tables and chairs with apparent ease.

The farmer's daughter hath soft brown hair;
  (*Butter and eggs and a pound of cheese*)
And I met with a ballad, I can't say where,
  Which wholly consisted of lines like these.

PART TWO

She sat with her hands 'neath her dimpled cheeks,
  (*Butter and eggs and a pound of cheese*)
And spake not a word.   While a lady speaks
  There is hope, but she didn't even sneeze.

She sat with her hands 'neath her crimson cheeks;
  (*Butter and eggs and a pound of cheese*)
She gave up mending her father's breeks,
  And let the cat roll in her best chemise.

She sat with her hands 'neath her burning cheeks,
  (*Butter and eggs and a pound of cheese*)
And gazed at the piper for thirteen weeks;
  Then she followed him out o'er the misty leas.

Her sheep followed her, as their tails did them,
  (*Butter and eggs and a pound of cheese*)
And this song is considered a perfect gem;
  And as to the meaning, it's what you please.

The Yarn of the Nancy Bell

W. S. GILBERT

Even this elderly naval man knows how to make effective use of a refrain!

T was on the shores that round our coast
   From Deal to Ramsgate span,
That I found alone on a piece of stone
   An elderly naval man.

His hair was weedy, his beard was long,
   And weedy and long was he;
And I heard this wight on the shore recite,
   In a singular minor key:

"Oh, I am a cook and a captain bold,
   And the mate of the Nancy brig,
And a bo'sun tight, and a midshipmite,
   And the crew of the captain's gig."

And he shook his fists and he tore his hair,
   Till I really felt afraid,
For I couldn't help thinking the man had been drinking,
   And so I simply said:

"Oh, elderly man, it's little I know
   Of the duties of men of the sea,
And I'll eat my hand if I understand
   However you can be

"At once a cook, and a captain bold,
   And the mate of the Nancy brig,
And a bo'sun tight, and a midshipmite,
   And the crew of the captain's gig."

Then he gave a hitch to his trousers, which
    Is a trick all seamen larn,
And having got rid of a thumping quid,
    He spun this painful yarn:

"'Twas in the good ship Nancy Bell
    That we sailed to the Indian Sea,
And there on a reef we came to grief,
    Which has often occurred to me.

"And pretty nigh all o' the crew was drowned
    (There was seventy-seven o' soul),
And only ten of the Nancy's men
    Said 'Here!' to the muster-roll.

"There was me and the cook and the captain bold,
    And the mate of the Nancy brig,
And a bo'sun tight, and a midshipmite,
    And the crew of the captain's gig.

"For a month we'd neither wittles nor drink,
    Till a-hungry we did feel.
So we drawed a lot, and accordin' shot
    The captain for our meal.

"The next lot fell to the Nancy's mate
    And a delicate dish he made;
Then our appetite with the midshipmite
    We seven survivors stayed.

"And then we murdered the bo'sun tight,
    And he much resembled pig;
Then we wittled free, did the cook and me,
    On the crew of the captain's gig.

"Then only the cook and me was left,
   And the delicate question, 'Which
Of us goes to the kettle?' arose,
   And we argued it out as sich.

"For I loved that cook as a brother, I did,
   And the cook he worshiped me;
But we'd both be blowed if we'd either be stowed
   In the other chap's hold, you see.

" 'I'll be eat if you dines off me,' says Tom;
   'Yes, that,' says I, 'you'll be; —
I'm boiled if I die, my friend,' quoth I;
   And 'Exactly so,' quoth he.

"Says he: 'Dear James, to murder me
   Were a foolish thing to do,
For don't you see that you can't cook *me*,
   While I can — and will — cook *you!*'

"So he boils the water, and takes the salt
   And the pepper in portions true
(Which he never forgot), and some chopped shalot,
   And some sage and parsley too.

" 'Come here,' says he, with a proper pride,
   Which his smiling features tell,
''T will soothing be if I let you see
   How extremely nice you'll smell.'

"And he stirred it round and round and round,
   And he sniffed at the foaming froth;
When I ups with his heels, and smothers his squeals
   In the scum of the boiling broth.

"And I eat that cook in a week or less,
  And — as I eating be
The last of his chops, why, I almost drops,
  For a wessel in sight I see!

        .   .   .   .   .

"And I never larf, and I never smile,
  And I never lark nor play;
But sit and croak, and a single joke
  I have — which is to say:

"Oh, I am a cook and a captain bold,
  And the mate of the Nancy brig.
And a bo'sun tight, and a midshipmite,
  And the crew of the captain's gig!"

IX: WORD MUSIC

"What's in a name?" says the scoffer. There is much in a name. Ask fathers and mothers why it is so difficult to choose names for babies. Ask little girls why one name won't do as well as another for doll or kitten. Ask any boy who has ever owned a dog and had the privilege of naming it!

Some words are pretty, and some are ugly. Some fit the things to which they are applied. Others are such misfits that they are amusing — like the small girl's "Snowball," which turned out to be a black and tan terrier.

The poet selects words with special care. It is not enough that they should convey the proper meaning. They must harmonize with the music of his verse. For poetry, as someone has said, is music which has been given the power of speech.

The sounds of which words are made have different qualities. The tones of some are loud and harsh. Others are soft and smooth. Some words whisper. Some hiss like a snake.

When the poet says, "Like steps of passing ghosts," one can almost hear in the syllables themselves the stir of ghostly feet. And when another poet speaks of

> The moan of doves in immemorial elms
> And murmuring of innumerable bees,

the ear recognizes in the music of the lines the low calls that mourning doves make, and the droning of honey-laden bees in summer air.

Word music is not always soothing and sweet. Listen to this:

> The terrible grumble and rumble and roar,
> Telling the battle was on once more!

[197]

And do you remember the noise of the highwayman's riding? —

> Over the cobbles he clattered and clashed in
> the dark inn yard.

Soft, melodious tones are not always suitable. Who would want a narrative of adventure to read like a lullaby? The sounds of syllables are sometimes as clashing and clamorous as the notes of a trumpet.

There are two or three ways in which the poet enhances the music of his verse. One of these is *alliteration*. Words are in alliteration when they begin with the same consonant sound: loud laugh; bad boy. Old English verse, hundreds of years ago, depended for its music almost entirely upon alliteration, or beginning rhyme, as it is sometimes called to distinguish it from end rhyme.

How pleasing are the *s* sounds in alliteration in this line:

> And snowy summits old in story;

and the *l*'s and *r*'s in this:

> With lisp of leaves and ripple of rain.

In the following quotation the alliterative *b* seems to bump like the clumsy beetle:

> The beetle booms adown the glooms
> And bumps along the dusk.

Another element in word music is *assonance*. Assonance is the repetition of the same vowel sound in words that do not rhyme: late, came; old story; firefly.

The assonance of the short *i*'s makes this a pretty line:

> It dips its misty light.

The recurring sound of long *o* makes this line melodious:

> From the molten-golden notes.

[198]

And notice how often and with what pleasant effect the sound of short *e* recurs in these sixteen words:

> Hear the sledges with the bells,
> > Silver bells!
> What a world of merriment their melody foretells!

It suggests the sound of a mandolin string pricked lightly several times in succession.

The music that comes from alliteration and assonance is not so easy to detect as that of rhyme. It requires practice to hear the delicate interweaving of sounds of which word music is made. Sometimes a poet becomes so interested in his thought that he forgets his music. When he does, his verse loses in beauty.

The Bells

EDGAR ALLAN POE

The music of the syllables is like an echo of the bells themselves. First comes the thin, silvery tinkle of sleigh bells. Then the wedding bells ring out in full chime, rich and golden. Suddenly the brass fire bells break into clashing jangle, so swift and terrifying that the very air seems to tremble. Last of all, the great iron bells begin their monotonous tolling — slow, muffled, and heavy.

I

Hear the sledges with the bells,
    Silver bells!
What a world of merriment their melody foretells!
    How they tinkle, tinkle, tinkle,
      In the icy air of night!
    While the stars that oversprinkle
    All the heavens seem to twinkle
      With a crystalline delight;
     Keeping time, time, time,
     In a sort of Runic rhyme,
To the tintinnabulation that so musically wells
   From the bells, bells, bells, bells,
     Bells, bells, bells —
From the jingling and the tinkling of the bells.

II

Hear the mellow wedding bells,
    Golden bells!
What a world of happiness their harmony foretells!
    Through the balmy air of night
    How they ring out their delight!

From the molten-golden notes,
    And all in tune,
  What a liquid ditty floats
To the turtledove that listens, while she gloats
    On the moon!
  Oh, from out the sounding cells,
What a gush of euphony voluminously wells!
    How it swells!
    How it dwells
  On the future; how it tells
  Of the rapture that impels
  To the swinging and the ringing
    Of the bells, bells, bells,
    Of the bells, bells, bells, bells,
      Bells, bells, bells —
To the rhyming and the chiming of the bells!

III

  Hear the loud alarum bells,
    Brazen bells!
What a tale of terror, now, their turbulency tells!
  In the startled ear of night
  How they scream out their affright!
    Too much horrified to speak,
    They can only shriek, shriek,
      Out of tune,
In a clamorous appealing to the mercy of the fire,
In a mad expostulation with the deaf and frantic fire.
  Leaping higher, higher, higher,
  With a desperate desire,
    And a resolute endeavor
    Now, now to sit, or never,
  By the side of the pale-faced moon.

Oh, the bells, bells, bells!
What a tale their terror tells
Of despair!
How they clang, and clash, and roar!
What a horror they outpour
On the bosom of the palpitating air!
Yet the ear it fully knows,
By the twanging,
And the clanging,
How the danger ebbs and flows;
Yet the ear distinctly tells,
In the jangling,
And the wrangling,
How the danger sinks and swells,
By the sinking or the swelling in the anger of the bells;
Of the bells
Of the bells, bells, bells, bells,
Bells, bells, bells —
In the clamor and the clangor of the bells!

IV

Hear the tolling of the bells,
Iron bells!
What a world of solemn thought their melody compels!
In the silence of the night
How we shiver with affright
At the melancholy menace of their tone!
For every sound that floats
From the rust within their throats
Is a groan.
And the people — ah, the people,
They that dwell up in the steeple,
All alone,

And who tolling, tolling, tolling,
    In that muffled monotone,
Feel a glory in so rolling
    On the human heart a stone —
They are neither man nor woman,
They are neither brute nor human,
        They are ghouls:
And their king it is who tolls;
And he rolls, rolls, rolls,
        Rolls
A paean from the bells!
And his merry bosom swells
With the paean of the bells!
And he dances, and he yells;
    Keeping time, time, time,
    In a sort of Runic rhyme,
To the paean of the bells,
        Of the bells;
    Keeping time, time, time,
    In a sort of Runic rhyme,
To the throbbing of the bells;
Of the bells, bells, bells —
To the sobbing of the bells;
    Keeping time, time, time,
As he knells, knells, knells,
In a happy Runic rhyme,
    To the rolling of the bells;
    Of the bells, bells, bells —
    To the tolling of the bells,
Of the bells, bells, bells, bells,
        Bells, bells, bells —
To the moaning and the groaning of the bells.

Four Little Foxes

Lew Sarett

The sound of these verses suggests the tones of a mother's voice as she comforts and soothes her frightened children.

Speak gently, Spring, and make no sudden sound;
For in my windy valley, yesterday I found
New-born foxes squirming on the ground —
     Speak gently.

Walk gently, March; forbear the bitter blow;
Her feet within a trap, her blood upon the snow,
The four little foxes saw their mother go —
     Walk softly.

Go lightly, Spring; oh, give them no alarm;
When I covered them with boughs to shelter them
    from harm,
The thin blue foxes suckled at my arm —
     Go lightly.

Step softly, March, with your rampant hurricane;
Nuzzling one another, and whimpering with pain,
The new little foxes are shivering in the rain —
     Step softly.

The Listeners

Walter de la Mare

In reading this poem, you discover that it has a soft and swishing music like a quiet breeze astir in a forest or footsteps hushed in fallen leaves. . . . Who the Traveler was, and whence he had come; and who the phantom listeners in the lone house far in the forest — these are questions the wandering moon might answer, or your own imagination!

Is there anybody there?" said the Traveler,
  Knocking on the moonlit door;
And his horse in the silence champed the grasses
  Of the forest's ferny floor:
And a bird flew up out of the turret,
  Above the Traveler's head:
And he smote upon the door again a second time;
  "Is there anybody there?" he said.
But no one descended to the Traveler;
  No head from the leaf-fringed sill
Leaned over and looked into his gray eyes,
  Where he stood perplexed and still.
But only a host of phantom listeners
  That dwelt in the lone house then
Stood listening in the quiet of the moonlight
  To that voice from the world of men:
Stood thronging the faint moonbeams on the dark stair,
  That goes down to the empty hall,
Hearkening in an air stirred and shaken
  By the lonely Traveler's call.
And he felt in his heart their strangeness,
  Their stillness answering his cry,

While his horse moved, cropping the dark turf,
   'Neath the starred and leafy sky;
For he suddenly smote on the door, even
   Louder, and lifted his head: —
"Tell them I came, and no one answered,
   That I kept my word," he said.
Never the least stir made the listeners,
   Though every word he spake
Fell echoing through the shadowiness of the still house
   From the one man left awake:
Aye, they heard his foot upon the stirrup,
   And the sound of iron on stone,
And how the silence surged softly backward,
   When the plunging hoofs were gone.

Spring Song

ALGERNON CHARLES SWINBURNE

Alliteration and assonance give this song a delicate melody.

For winter's rains and ruins are over,
   And all the season of snows and sins;
The days dividing lover and lover,
   The light that loses, the night that wins;
And time remembered is grief forgotten,
And frosts are slain and flowers begotten,
And in green underwood and cover
   Blossom by blossom the spring begins.

Scythe Song

ANDREW LANG

The poem imitates the hushed sound of the scythe, swinging through deep-grown clover and grass.

Mowers, weary and brown, and blithe,
   What is the word methinks ye know,
Endless over-word that the Scythe
   Sings to the blades of the grass below?
Scythes that swing in the grass and clover,
   Something, still, they say as they pass;
What is the word that, over and over,
   Sings the Scythe to the flowers and grass?

Hush, ah hush, the Scythes are saying,
   Hush, and heed not, and fall asleep;
Hush, they say to the grasses swaying,
   Hush, they sing to the clover deep!
Hush — 'tis the lullaby Time is singing —
   Hush, and heed not, for all things pass,
Hush, ah hush! and the Scythes are swinging
   Over the clover, over the grass!

How They Brought the Good News from Ghent to Aix

ROBERT BROWNING

The rhythm of galloping horses would not be suitable to delicate music, but it is suitable to the vigorous sounding words of this poem.

I sprang to the stirrup, and Joris, and he;
I galloped, Dirck galloped, we galloped all three;
"Good speed!" cried the watch, as the gate-bolts undrew;
"Speed!" echoed the wall to us galloping through;
Behind shut the postern, the lights sank to rest,
And into the midnight we galloped abreast.

Not a word to each other; we kept the great pace
Neck by neck, stride by stride, never changing our place;
I turned in my saddle and made its girths tight,
Then shortened each stirrup, and set the pique right,
Rebuckled the cheek-strap, chained slacker the bit,
Nor galloped less steadily Roland a whit.

'Twas moonset at starting; but while we drew near
Lokeren, the cocks crew and twilight dawned clear;
At Boom, a great yellow star came out to see;
At Düffeld, 'twas morning as plain as could be;
And from Mecheln church steeple we heard the half chime,
So Joris broke silence with, "Yet there is time!"

At Aerschot, up leaped of a sudden the sun,
And against him the cattle stood black every one,
To stare through the mist at us galloping past,
And I saw my stout galloper Roland at last,
With resolute shoulders, each butting away
The haze, as some bluff river headland its spray:

And his low head and crest — just one sharp ear bent back
For my voice, and the other pricked out on his track;
And one eye's black intelligence, — ever that glance
O'er its white edge at me, his own master, askance!
And the thick heavy spume-flakes which aye and anon
His fierce lips shook upwards in galloping on.

By Hasselt, Dirck groaned; and cried Joris, "Stay spur!
Your Roos galloped bravely, the fault's not in her,
We'll remember at Aix" — for one heard the quick wheeze
Of her chest, saw the stretched neck and staggering knees,
And sunk tail, and horrible heave of the flank,
As down on her haunches she shuddered and sank.

So we were left galloping, Joris and I,
Past Looz and past Tongres, no cloud in the sky;
The broad sun above laughed a pitiless laugh,
'Neath our feet broke the brittle bright stubble like chaff;
Till over by Dalhem a dome-spire sprang white,
And "Gallop," gasped Joris, "for Aix is in sight!

"How they'll greet us!" — and all in a moment his roan
Rolled neck and croup over, lay dead as a stone;
And there was my Roland to bear the whole weight
Of the news which alone could save Aix from her fate,
With his nostrils like pits full of blood to the brim,
And with circles of red for his eye-sockets' rim.

Then I cast loose my buffcoat, each holster let fall,
Shook off my jack-boots, let go belt and all,
Stood up in the stirrup, leaned, patted his ear,
Called my Roland his pet name, my horse without peer;
Clapped my hands, laughed and sang, any noise, bad or
     good,
Till at length into Aix Roland galloped and stood.

And all I remember is — friends flocking round
As I sat with his head 'twixt my knees on the ground;
And no voice but was praising this Roland of mine,
As I poured down his throat our last measure of wine,
Which (the burgesses voted by common consent)
Was no more than his due who brought good news from
     Ghent.

Song in the Songless

GEORGE MEREDITH

*Can you not hear in the s's the sighing sound of withered sedges
shaken by the wind?*

They have no song, the sedges dry,
   And still they sing.
It is within my heart they sing,
   As I pass by.

Within my breast they touch a string,
   They wake a sigh.
There is but sound of sedges dry;
   In me they sing.

Song of the Chattahoochee

SIDNEY LANIER

Never a river sang sweeter music to listening flowers and trees than the swift-flowing river of this poem sings for you.

Out of the hills of Habersham,
Down the valleys of Hall,
I hurry amain to reach the plain,
Run the rapid and leap the fall,
Split at the rock and together again,
Accept my bed, or narrow or wide,
And flee from folly on every side
With a lover's pain to attain the plain
Far from the hills of Habersham,
Far from the valleys of Hall.

All down the hills of Habersham,
All through the valleys of Hall,
The rushes cried *Abide, abide,*
The willful waterweeds held me thrall,
The laving laurel turned my tide,
The ferns and the fondling grass said *Stay,*
The dewberry dipped for to work delay,
And the little reeds sighed *Abide, abide,*
Here in the hills of Habersham,
Here in the valleys of Hall.

High o'er the hills of Habersham,
Veiling the valleys of Hall,
The hickory told me manifold
Fair tales of shade, the poplar tall
Wrought me her shadowy self to hold,

The chestnut, the oak, the walnut, the pine,
Overleaning, with flickering meaning and sign,
Said, *Pass not, so cold, these manifold*
   Deep shades of the hills of Habersham,
   These glades in the valleys of Hall.

   And oft in the hills of Habersham,
   And oft in the valleys of Hall,
The white quartz shone, and the smooth brook-stone
Did bar me of passage with friendly brawl,
And many a luminous jewel lone
— Crystals clear or a-cloud with mist,
Ruby, garnet, and amethyst —
Made lures with the lights of streaming stone
   In the clefts of the hills of Habersham,
   In the beds of the valleys of Hall.

   But oh, not the hills of Habersham,
   And oh, not the valleys of Hall
Avail: I am fain for to water the plain.
Downward the voices of Duty call —
Downward, to toil and be mixed with the main.
The dry fields burn, and the mills are to turn,
And a myriad flowers mortally yearn,
And the lordly main from beyond the plain
   Calls o'er the Hills of Habersham,
   Calls through the valleys of Hall.

Annabel Lee

EDGAR ALLAN POE

Like many of Poe's poems, this one is almost pure music.

It was many and many a year ago,
  In a kingdom by the sea,
That a maiden there lived whom you may know
  By the name of Annabel Lee;
And this maiden she lived with no other thought
  Than to love and be loved by me.

I was a child and she was a child,
  In this kingdom by the sea
But we loved with a love that was more than love,
  I and my Annabel Lee;
With a love that the wingéd seraphs of heaven
  Coveted her and me.

And this was the reason that, long ago,
  In this kingdom by the sea,
A wind blew out of a cloud, chilling
  My beautiful Annabel Lee;
So that her highborn kinsmen came
  And bore her away from me,
To shut her up in a sepulcher
  In this kingdom by the sea.

The angels, not half so happy in heaven,
  Went envying her and me;
Yes! that was the reason (as all men know,
  In this kingdom by the sea)
That the wind came out of the cloud by night,
  Chilling and killing my Annabel Lee.

But our love it was stronger by far than the love
　　Of those who were older than we,
　　Of many far wiser than we;
And neither the angels in heaven above,
　　Nor the demons down under the sea,
Can ever dissever my soul from the soul
　　Of the beautiful Annabel Lee:

For the moon never beams, without bringing me dreams
　　Of the beautiful Annabel Lee;
And the stars never rise, but I feel the bright eyes
　　Of the beautiful Annabel Lee;
And so, all the night-tide, I lie down by the side
Of my darling — my darling — my life and my bride,
　　In her sepulcher there by the sea,
　　In her tomb by the sounding sea.

Bugle Song

ALFRED, LORD TENNYSON

In the first stanza the sound of the bugle is full and round. Later, as the blast fades in the distance and the echoes come floating back, the sounds of the words grow thinner and softer, in imitation of the echo.

The splendor falls on castle walls
  And snowy summits old in story:
The long light shakes across the lakes,
  And the wild cataract leaps in glory.
Blow, bugle, blow, set the wild echoes flying,
Blow, bugle; answer, echoes, dying, dying, dying.

O hark, O hear! how thin and clear,
  And thinner, clearer, farther going!
O sweet and far from cliff and scar
  The horns of Elfland faintly blowing!
Blow, let us hear the purple glens replying:
Blow, bugle; answer, echoes, dying, dying, dying.

O love, they die in yon rich sky,
  They faint on hill or field or river:
Our echoes roll from soul to soul,
  And grow for ever and for ever.
Blow, bugle, blow, set the wild echoes flying,
And answer, echoes, answer, dying, dying, dying.

The Beetle

JAMES WHITCOMB RILEY

Through the varying sounds of the summer night the blundering beetle bumps his way.

The shrilling locust slowly sheathes
His dagger-voice, and creeps away
Beneath the brooding leaves where breathes
The zephyr of the dying day:
One naked star has waded through
The purple shallows of the night,
And faltering as falls the dew
It drips its misty light.
    O'er garden blooms,
    On tides of musk,
    The beetle booms adown the glooms
    And bumps along the dusk.

The katydid is rasping at
The silence from the tangled broom:
On drunken wings the flitting bat
Goes staggering athwart the gloom:
The toadstool bulges through the weeds;
And lavishly to left and right
The fireflies, like golden seeds,
Are sown about the night.
    O'er slumbrous blooms,
    On floods of musk,
    The beetle booms adown the glooms
    And bumps along the dusk.

The primrose flares its baby hands
Wide open, as the empty moon,
Slow lifted from the underlands,
Drifts up the azure-arched lagoon:
The shadows on the garden walk
Are frayed with rifts of silver light:
And trickling down the poppy stalk,
The dewdrop streaks the night.
  O'er folded blooms,
  On swirls of musk,
  The beetle booms adown the glooms
  And bumps along the dusk.

White Butterflies

ALGERNON CHARLES SWINBURNE

These stanzas have as soft a sound as breathing, as gentle a movement as the wings of butterflies.

Fly, white butterflies, out to sea,
Frail, pale wings for the wind to try,
Small white wings that we scarce can see,
  Fly!

Some fly light as a laugh of glee,
Some fly soft as a long, low sigh;
All to the haven where each would be,
  Fly!

Border Ballad

SIR WALTER SCOTT

The Blue Bonnets are gathering from the Border districts, from Ettrick to Liddesdale, to do battle for their queen. Can you hear through the rhythm the quick trampling of many feet? These Scotch clansmen do not march forward in even rank, but hurry and crowd in their eagerness.

March, march, Ettrick and Teviotdale;
 Why the de'il dinna ye march forward in order?
March, march, Eskdale and Liddesdale,
 All the Blue Bonnets are bound for the Border!
  Many a banner spread
  Flutters above your head,
Many a crest that is famous in story.
  Mount and make ready then,
  Sons of the mountain glen,
Fight for the Queen and our old Scottish glory.

Come from the hills where your hirsels are grazing;
 Come from the glen of the buck and the roe;
Come to the crag where the beacon is blazing;
 Come with the buckler, the lance, and the bow.
  Trumpets are sounding,
  War steeds are bounding;
Stand to your arms, then, and march in good order.
  England shall many a day
  Tell of the bloody fray,
When the Blue Bonnets came over the Border.

Ellen McJones Aberdeen

W. S. GILBERT

You've only to listen to the sound of the bagpiper's name to know that the Englishman who wrote this did not like bagpipes. Have you ever heard so many discordant syllables as there are in these verses?

Macphairson Clonglocketty Angus McClan
Was the son of an elderly laboring man;
You've guessed him a Scotchman, shrewd reader, at sight,
And p'r'haps altogether, shrewd reader, you're right.

From the bonnie blue Forth to the beastly Deeside,
Round by Dingwall and Wrath to the mouth of the Clyde,
There wasn't a child or woman or man
Who could pipe with Clonglocketty Angus McClan.

No other could wake such detestable groans,
With reed and with chaunter — with bag and with drones:
All day and all night he delighted the chiels
With sniggering pibrochs and jiggety reels.

He'd clamber a mountain and squat on the ground,
And the neighboring maidens would gather around
To list to his pipes and to gaze in his een,
Especially Ellen McJones Aberdeen.

All loved their McClan, save a Sassenach brute,
Who came to the Highlands to fish and to shoot;
He dressed himself up in a Highlander way;
Though his name it was Pattison Corby Torbay.

Torbay had incurred a good deal of expense
To make him a Scotchman in every sense;
But this is a matter, you'll readily own,
That isn't a question of tailors alone.

A Sassenach chief may be bonily built,
He may purchase a sporran, a bonnet, and kilt;
Stick a skean in his hose — wear an acre of stripes —
But he cannot assume an affection for pipes.

Clonglocketty's pipings all night and all day
Quite frenzied poor Pattison Corby Torbay;
The girls were amused at his singular spleen,
Especially Ellen McJones Aberdeen.

"Macphairson Clonglocketty Angus, my lad,
With pibrochs and reels you are driving me mad.
If you really must play on that cursed affair,
My goodness! play something resembling an air."

Boiled over, the blood of Macphairson McClan —
The Clan of Clonglocketty rose as one man;
For all were enraged at the insult, I ween —
Especially Ellen McJones Aberdeen.

"Let's show," said McClan, "to this Sassenach loon
That the bagpipes *can* play him a regular tune.
Let's see," said McClan, as he thoughtfully sat,
" 'In My Cottage' is easy — I'll practice at that."

He blew at his "Cottage," and blew with a will,
For a year, seven months, and a fortnight, until
(You'll hardly believe it!) McClan, I declare,
Elicited something resembling an air.

It was wild — it was fitful — as wild as the breeze —
It wandered about into several keys;
It was jerky, spasmodic, and harsh, I'm aware,
But still it distinctly suggested an air!

The Sassenach screamed, and the Sassenach danced;
He shrieked in his agony — bellowed and pranced;
And the maidens who gathered rejoiced at the scene,
Especially Ellen McJones Aberdeen.

"Hech gather, hech gather, hech gather around,
And fill a' ye lugs wi' the exquisite sound.
An air fra' the bagpipes — beat that if ye can:
Hurrah for Clonglocketty Angus McClan!"

The fame of his piping spread over the land;
Respectable widows proposed for his hand,
And maidens came flocking to sit on the green —
Especially Ellen McJones Aberdeen.

One morning the fidgety Sassenach swore
He'd stand it no longer — he drew his claymore,
And (this was, I think, extremely bad taste)
Divided Clonglocketty close to the waist.

Oh! loud were the wailings for Angus McClan,
Oh! deep was the grief for that excellent man —
The maids stood aghast at the horrible scene,
Especially Ellen McJones Aberdeen.

It sorrowed poor Pattison Corby Torbay
To find them "take on" in this serious way;
He pitied the poor little fluttering birds,
And solaced their souls with the following words: —

"Oh, maidens," said Pattison, touching his hat,
"Don't blubber, my dears, for a fellow like that;
Observe, I'm a very superior man,
A much better fellow than Angus McClan."

They smiled when he winked and addressed them as
    "dears,"
And they all of them vowed, as they dried up their tears,
A pleasanter gentleman never was seen —
Especially Ellen McJones Aberdeen.

The *chaunter* is the shrill pipe in a bagpipe, and the *drone* is the large tube which makes the deep, droning sound. The *pibroch* is wild music played on the bagpipe. *Chiels* means young lads and maidens; *Sassenach* (Saxon), an Englishman. A *sporran* is the fur pouch worn by Highlanders in front of the kilt, and a *skean* is a knife or dagger.

Ko-Ko's Song

W. S. GILBERT

Here is alliteration, indeed, and assonance too! Surely the rhymester isn't making fun of poor Ko-Ko?

There is beauty in the bellow of the blast,
    There is grandeur in the growing of the gale,
        There is eloquent outpouring
        When the lion is a-roaring,
    And the tiger is a-lashing of his tail!

        Yes, I like to see a tiger
        From the Congo or the Niger,
    And especially when lashing of his tail!

To Sea, To Sea!

THOMAS LOVELL BEDDOES

*These syllables ring sharp and clear.   They rise and fall with a strong,
firm rhythm, like the movement of a great sailing vessel over the billows.*

To sea, to sea!   The calm is o'er;
　The wanton water leaps in sport,
And rattles down the pebbly shore;
　The dolphin wheels, the sea-cows snort,
And unseen mermaids' pearly song
Comes bubbling up, the weeds among.
　Fling broad the sail, dip deep the oar:
　To sea, to sea!   the calm is o'er.

To sea, to sea!   our wide-winged bark
　Shall billowy cleave its sunny way,
And with its shadow, fleet and dark,
　Break the caved Tritons' azure day,
Like mighty eagle soaring light
O'er antelopes on Alpine height.
　The anchor heaves, the ship swings free,
　The sails swell full.   To sea, to sea!

SO·HE·THINKS·HE·SHALL·TAKE·TO·THE·SEA·AGAIN
FOR·ONE·MORE·CRUISE·WITH·HIS·BUCCANEERS

X: PICTURES IN POETRY

Aladdin's lamp was shattered long ago. Lost are the words which opened a door into the magic mountain.

And still, so long as there are words and poets to use them, who will say there is no magic? The poet dips his pen into a bottle of ink, and lo! —

Daffodils shine like living gold along the margin of a lake. . . . A pale star rises in the East for watching herds and flocks to see. . . . In a crowded city street, a little lost puppy shivers with cold and fear. . . . And side by side, under a dripping forest tree, a man and wolf seek shelter together.

The poet is a painter. His keen sight discovers interesting details which we had not before observed. He points out beauty in commonplace things that we had overlooked. No matter whether you like dogs or not, you can't help sharing with the poet this dog's joy in snow:

> and now with many a frisk
> Wide-scampering, snatches up the drifted snow
> With ivory teeth, or plows it with his snout;
> Then shakes his powdered coat and barks for joy.

Because he paints to the imagination, and because the imagination travels farther than feet can ever go, the poet can show us things that, without him, we might never see. His words recapture the living image of the little Revenge, her torn sails flying bravely between the double battle-line of the towering Armada. We look down with him from the eagle's height among the clouds to see how

> The wrinkled sea beneath him crawls.

Or he may even carry us in imagination to another world than this, a world of haunting beauty which we glimpse through

> magic casements, opening on the foam
> Of perilous seas, in faery lands forlorn.

The poet's pictures are more than paintings.   They have movement as well as light and color.

> When all at once I saw a crowd,
> A host, of golden daffodils;
> Beside the lake, beneath the trees,
> Fluttering and dancing in the breeze.

Poetic imagery has sound, too, and feeling.   As you read these lines, you not only see the storm, but you hear it,

> Bending the props of the pine-tree roof,
> And snapping many a rafter.

You feel the wolf's body pushing against yours, as did the poet:

> His wet fur pressed against me;
> Each of us warmed the other.

So great is the power of suggestion which words possess that they seem able even to revive odors.   The pure fragrance of the lily and the tallowy smell of burning candles linger in these lines.

> Sweet is the lily's silver bell,
> And sweet the wakeful tapers' smell
> That watch for early prayer.

One of the greatest pleasures in reading poetry comes from the vivid pictures it creates.   Even though one's outward eyes should become blind and darkened, the poet's pictures would still "flash upon that inward eye" of memory and imagination.

Little Lost Pup

ARTHUR GUITERMAN

*It may be hard to decide which is the more effective picture, that of the little
pup lost or found; but there is no doubt which is the happier.*

He was lost! — not a shade of doubt of that;
For he never barked at a slinking cat,
But stood in the square where the wind blew raw,
With a drooping ear and a trembling paw
And a mournful look in his pleading eye
And a plaintive sniff at the passer-by
That begged as plain as a tongue could sue,
"O Mister! please may I follow you?"
A lorn, wee waif of a tawny brown
Adrift in the roar of a heedless town —
Ah, the saddest of sights in a world of sin
Is a little lost pup with his tail tucked in!

Well, he won my heart (for I set great store
On my own red Bute — who is here no more),
So I whistled clear, and he trotted up,
And who so glad as that small lost pup!
Now he shares my board, and he owns my bed,
And he fairly shouts when he hears my tread;
Then, if things go wrong, as they sometimes do,
And the world is cold and I'm feeling blue,
He asserts his right to assuage my woes
With a warm red tongue and a nice cold nose
And a silky head on my arm or knee
And a paw as soft as a paw can be.

When we rove the woods for a league about,
He's as full of pranks as a school let out;
For he romps and frisks like a three-months' colt,
And he runs me down like a thunderbolt.
Oh, the blithest of sights in the world so fair
Is a gay little pup with his tail in the air!

The Woodman's Dog

WILLIAM COWPER

If you have ever watched a dog playing in the snow, then you know how realistic these details are.

Shaggy, and lean, and shrewd, with pointed ears
And tail cropped short, half lurcher and half cur —
His dog attends him.   Close behind his heel
Now creeps he slow; and now with many a frisk
Wide-scampering, snatches up the drifted snow
With ivory teeth, or plows it with his snout;
Then shakes his powdered coat and barks for joy.

Daffodils

WILLIAM WORDSWORTH

Countless people who have never traveled there have seen the golden fields of daffodils in Wordsworth's England.

I wandered lonely as a cloud
That floats on high o'er vales and hills,
When all at once I saw a crowd,
A host, of golden daffodils;
Beside the lake, beneath the trees,
Fluttering and dancing in the breeze.

Continuous as the stars that shine
And twinkle on the Milky Way,
They stretched in never-ending line
Along the margin of a bay:
Ten thousand saw I at a glance,
Tossing their heads in sprightly dance.

The waves beside them danced, but they
Outdid the sparkling waves in glee:
A poet could not but be gay,
In such a jocund company:
I gazed — and gazed — but little thought
What wealth the show to me had brought:

For oft, when on my couch I lie
In vacant or in pensive mood,
They flash upon that inward eye
Which is the bliss of solitude;
And then my heart with pleasure fills,
And dances with the daffodils.

A Dutch Picture

Henry Wadsworth Longfellow

Here are enough colorful pictures, Dutch and Spanish, for a great frieze.

Simon Danz has come home again,
  From cruising about with his buccaneers;
He has singed the beard of the King of Spain,
And carried away the Dean of Jaen
  And sold him in Algiers.

In his house by the Maese, with its roof of tiles,
  And weathercocks flying aloft in air,
There are silver tankards of antique styles,
Plunder of convent and castle, and piles
  Of carpets rich and rare.

In his tulip garden there by the town,
  Overlooking the sluggish stream,
With his Moorish cap and dressing gown,
The old sea-captain, hale and brown,
Walks in a waking dream.

A smile in his gray mustachio lurks
  Whenever he thinks of the King of Spain;
And the listed tulips look like Turks,
And the silent gardener as he works
  Is changed to the Dean of Jaen.

The windmills on the outermost
  Verge of the landscape in the haze,
To him are towers on the Spanish coast,
With whiskered sentinels at their post,
  Though this is the river Maese.

But when the winter rains begin,
    He sits and smokes by the blazing brands,
And old seafaring men come in,
Goat-bearded, gray, and with double chin,
    And rings upon their hands.

They sit there in the shadow and shine
    Of the flickering fire of the winter night;
Figures in color and design
Like those by Rembrandt of the Rhine,
    Half darkness and half light.

And they talk of ventures lost or won,
    And their talk is ever and ever the same,
While they drink the red wine of Tarragon,
From the cellars of some Spanish Don,
    Or convent set on flame.

Restless at times with heavy strides
    He paces his parlor to and fro;
He is like a ship that at anchor rides,
And swings with the rising and falling tides,
    And tugs at her anchor tow.

Voices mysterious far and near,
    Sound of the wind and sound of the sea,
Are calling and whispering in his ear,
"Simon Danz!   Why stayest thou here?
    Come forth and follow me!"

So he thinks he shall take to the sea again
    For one more cruise with his buccaneers,
To singe the beard of the King of Spain,
And capture another Dean of Jaen
    And sell him in Algiers.

To a Black Dog, Bereaved

Elizabeth Coatsworth

He is an appealing little figure, this black young dog, as he looks so eagerly for the playfellow who will not come again.

Unless that kitty shines again in heaven,
  She is forever lost.
It is in vain you dart around each corner:
  You seek a ghost.

Oh, you may stand, eyes shining, one paw lifted,
  Tense to the ultimate hair.
Your expectation is but effort wasted:
  She is not there.

A shadow you may move, your tail just wagging,
  Scenting each breeze,
But she is less than shadow and her spirit
  Haunts not our trees.

Never again shall I (I fear) behold her
  In mimic flight,
Gold as the sun, with you pursuing after
  As day flees night.

A Story for a Child

BAYARD TAYLOR

Because of the clarity of its pictures, this narrative keeps the flavor of excitement which the real adventure had.

Little one, come to my knee!
  Hark, how the rain is pouring
Over the roof, in the pitch-black night,
  And the wind in the woods a-roaring!

Hush, my darling, and listen,
  Then pay for the story with kisses;
Father was lost in the pitch-black night,
  In just such a storm as this is!

High up on the lonely mountains,
  Where the wild men watched and waited;
Wolves in the forest, and bears in the bush,
  And I on my path belated.

The rain and the night together
  Came down, and the wind came after,
Bending the props of the pine-tree roof,
  And snapping many a rafter.

I crept along in the darkness,
  Stunned, and bruised, and blinded, —
Crept to a fir with thick-set boughs,
  And a sheltering rock behind it.

There, from the blowing and raining,
  Crouching, I sought to hide me:
Something rustled, two green eyes shone,
  And a wolf lay down beside me.

Little one, be not frightened;
    I and the wolf together,
Side by side, through the long, long night
    Hid from the awful weather.

His wet fur pressed against me;
    Each of us warmed the other;
Each of us felt, in the stormy dark,
    That beast and man were brother.

And when the falling forest
    No longer crashed in warning,
Each of us went from our hiding place
    Forth in the wild, wet morning.

Darling, kiss me in payment!
    Hark, how the wind is roaring;
Father's house is a better place
    When the stormy rain is pouring!

Romance

ANDREW LANG

The colors of these pictures are as soft and delicate as those reflected in a clear forest pool.

My Love dwelt in a northern land.
  A gray tower in a forest green
Was hers, and far on either hand
  The long wash of the waves was seen,
And leagues and leagues of yellow sand,
  The woven forest boughs between!

And through the silver northern night
  The sunset slowly died away,
And herds of strange deer, lily-white,
  Stole forth among the branches gray;
About the coming of the light,
  They fled like ghosts before the day!

I know not if the forest green
  Still girdles round the castle gray;
I know not if the boughs between
  The white deer vanish ere the day;
Above my Love the grass is green,
  My heart is colder than the day.

The Deserted House

Mary Coleridge

*Is there anything more lonesome than a deserted house? Even the
birds seem to shun this one.*

There's no smoke in the chimney,
    And the rain beats on the floor;
There's no glass in the window,
    There's no wood in the door;
And heather grows behind the house,
    And the sand lies before.

No hand hath trained the ivy,
    The walls are gray and bare;
The boats upon the sea sail by,
    Nor never tarry there.
No beast of the field comes nigh,
    Nor any bird of the air.

Twelfth Night Carol

On Twelfth Night Eve little bands of carol singers used to go from door to door in Old England. This carol suggests a sketch for a Christmas card.

Here we come a-whistling through the fields so green;
Here we come a-singing, so fair to be seen.
 God send you happy, God send you happy,
 Pray God send you a Happy New Year!

The roads are very dirty, our boots are very thin,
We have little pockets to put pennies in.
 God send you happy, God send you happy,
 Pray God send you a Happy New Year!

Bring out your little table and spread it with a cloth,
Bring out your jug of milk, likewise your Christmas loaf.
 God send you happy, God send you happy,
 Pray God send you a Happy New Year!

God bless the master of this house, God bless the mistress
  too;
And all the little children that round the table go.
 God send you happy, God send you happy,
 Pray God send you a Happy New Year!

WAITS' GREETING

Yuletide Fires

*Do you notice that this old song is done all in Christmas colors —
the burning log, the scarlet holly bough, and clear star-shine?*

Light with the burning log of oak
The darkness of thy care,
Deck with the scarlet-berried bough
The temple of the fair;
Spread pure white linen for a feast,
Perchance some guest may share.

Give forth thy gold and silver coins,
For they were lent to thee;
Put out to usury thy dross,
One talent gaineth three.
Perchance the hungered and the poor
May pray to God for thee.

Once a pale star arose in the East
For watching herds to see,
And weakness came to Bethlehem,
And strength to Galilee.
Perchance if thou dost keep thy tryst
A star may rise for thee.

AN OLD SONG

Winter

WILLIAM SHAKESPEARE

Here is a picture of winter indeed — Dick the shepherd blowing upon his finger nails to warm his hands; the kitchen maid Joan skimming the boiling pot; coughs drowning the parson's solemn sentences; frozen milk; red noses; birds shivering in the snow; and crab apples sizzling in hot cider. The poem is taken from the play, "Love's Labor's Lost."

When icicles hang by the wall,
    And Dick the shepherd blows his nail,
And Tom bears logs into the hall,
    And milk comes frozen home in pail,
When blood is nipped and ways be foul,
Then nightly sings the staring owl,
Tu-whit, tu-who! a merry note,
While greasy Joan doth keel the pot.

When all aloud the wind doth blow,
    And coughing drowns the parson's saw,
And birds sit brooding in the snow,
    And Marian's nose looks red and raw,
When roasted crabs hiss in the bowl,
Then nightly sings the staring owl,
Tu-whit, tu-who! a merry note,
While greasy Joan doth keel the pot.

Fairy Song

William Shakespeare

Although the fairy talks as if she is kept very busy, her tasks sound as light and graceful as the flying movement of the rhythm. The lines are from the play, "A Midsummer Night's Dream."

Over hill, over dale,
  Thorough bush, thorough brier,
Over park, over pale,
  Thorough flood, thorough fire,
I do wander everywhere,
Swifter than the moonë's sphere;
And I serve the fairy queen,
To dew her orbs upon the green.
The cowslips tall her pensioners be;
In their gold coats spots you see:
Those be rubies, fairy favors,
In those freckles live their savors.
I must go seek some dewdrops here,
And hang a pearl in every cowslip's ear.

No *pale*, or fence, can hinder the fairy in her tasks. The *orbs* which she sprinkles with dew are the dark green fairy-rings often seen in the grass of meadows. The queen's *pensioners* or gentlemen-at-arms, the tall golden cowslips, guard the fairies in their revels.

The Owl and the Pussy-Cat

EDWARD LEAR

If you take time really to look at these pictures, you will find them more amusing than any in the comic strip in the newspaper.

The Owl and the Pussy-cat went to sea
   In a beautiful pea-green boat:
They took some honey and plenty of money
   Wrapped up in a five-pound note.
The Owl looked up to the stars above,
   And sang to a small guitar,
"O lovely Pussy, O Pussy, my love,
   What a beautiful Pussy you are,
         You are,
         You are!
What a beautiful Pussy you are!"

Pussy said to the Owl, "You elegant fowl,
   How charmingly sweet you sing!
Oh! let us be married; too long we have tarried:
   But what shall we do for a ring?"
They sailed away for a year and a day,
   To the land where the bong-tree grows;
And there in a wood a Piggy-wig stood,
   With a ring at the end of his nose,
         His nose,
         His nose,
With a ring at the end of his nose.

"Dear Pig, are you willing to sell for one shilling
 Your ring?"   Said the Piggy, "I will."
So they took it away, and were married next day
 By the Turkey who lives on the hill.
They dined on mince and slices of quince,
 Which they ate with a runcible spoon;
And hand in hand, on the edge of the sand,
 They danced by the light of the moon,
            The moon,
            The moon,
 They danced by the light of the moon.

Shelter

Charles Stuart Calverley

The rhymester paints with such dainty, sentimental strokes that he makes you believe he is about to show you — what? In which line do you first suspect that he is teasing you?

By the wide lake's margin I marked her lie —
　　The wide, weird lake where the alders sigh —
A fair young thing, with a shy, soft eye;
　　And I deemed that her thoughts had flown
To her home, and her brethren, and sisters dear,
As she lay there watching the dark, deep mere,
　　All motionless, all alone.

Then I heard a noise, as of men and boys,
　　And a boisterous troop drew nigh.
Whither now will retreat those fairy feet?
　　Where hide till the storm pass by?
One glance — the wild glance of a hunted thing —
She cast behind her; she gave one spring;
And there followed a splash and a broadening ring
　　On the lake where the alders sigh.

She had gone from the ken of ungentle men!
　　Yet scarce did I mourn for that;
For I knew she was safe in her own home then,
And, the danger past, would appear again,
　　For she was a water rat.

When You Go to Fairyland

Of course she went there! How else could she know about the wild-rose cradles and the rabbit hole?

Once I went to Fairyland — but it's years and years ago—
I wandered through a dusky wood when the moon was
        shining low;
I saw the fairies dancing, and they made me join them too,
For when you go to Fairyland you must do as the fairies do.

The fairy queen was beautiful.   She wore a shimmery gown
All made of misty moonbeams, with star-shine in her crown:
The fairies bowed in front of her, so I made a curtsy too,
For when you go to Fairyland you must do as the fairies do.

I peeped at fairy babies in their wild-rose cradles sleeping,
And I watched them gently rocking when the cool night
        wind came creeping,
Then I perched on a crimson toadstool and I sipped some
        honey dew,
For when you go to Fairyland you must do as the fairies do.

They feasted me with fairy fruits and they gave me fairy
        gold,
But they all trooped down a rabbit hole when the night was
        growing old;
Oh, I *tried*, I *tried* to follow them, but I couldn't wriggle
        through,
So I came away, for in Fairyland you must do as the fairies
        do.

ANONYMOUS

[244]

Meeting at Night

ROBERT BROWNING

The quiet night seems astir with small noises, but in the bright light of morning the poet notices no sounds, only the splendor of the sun's path of gold on the sea.

The gray sea and the long black land;
And the yellow half-moon large and low;
And the startled little waves that leap
In fiery ringlets from their sleep,
As I gain the cove with pushing prow,
And quench its speed i' the slushy sand.

Then a mile of warm sea-scented beach;
Three fields to cross till a farm appears;
A tap at the pane, the quick sharp scratch
And blue spurt of a lighted match,
And a voice less loud, through its joys and fears,
Than the two hearts beating each to each!

Parting at Morning

Round the cape of a sudden came the sea,
And the sun looked over the mountain's rim;
And straight was a path of gold for him,
And the need of a world of men for me.

Music, When Soft Voices Die

PERCY BYSSHE SHELLEY

Lost loveliness lingers not only in the poet's memory but in the verses he leaves for our enjoyment.

Music, when soft voices die,
Vibrates in the memory;
Odors, when sweet violets sicken,
Live within the sense they quicken.

Rose leaves, when the rose is dead,
Are heaped for the beloved's bed;
And so thy thoughts, when thou art **gone,**
Love itself shall slumber on.

The Forsaken Merman

MATTHEW ARNOLD

Long ago people held a quaint belief in mermen and mermaids. Sometimes, they thought, a mortal married one and went to live in the wild sea-caves. But whoever married a merman would lose her soul and be barred from the gates of Heaven unless she forsook him and returned to her own people and her own church.

In this poem a merman is speaking. On a clear, moonlight night he and his gold-haired children rise from the sea to call the mortal mother who has forsaken them. They cannot believe that she will return no more.

There are few poems in the English language with such varied and picturesque imagery as this.

Come, dear children, let us away;
    Down and away below!
Now my brothers call from the bay;
Now the great winds shoreward blow;
Now the salt tides seaward flow;
Now the wild white horses play,
Champ and chafe and toss in the spray.
    Children dear, let us away!
      This way, this way!

Call her once before you go —
    Call once yet
In a voice that she will know:
    "Margaret! Margaret!"
Children's voices should be dear
(Call once more) to a mother's ear;
Children's voices, wild with pain —
Surely she will come again.

Call her once and come away;
    This way, this way!
"Mother dear, we cannot stay.
The wild white horses foam and fret."
    Margaret! Margaret!

Come, dear children, come away down;
    Call no more!
One last look at the white-walled town,
And the little gray church on the windy shore;
    Then come down.
She will not come though you call all day;
    Come away, come away!

Children dear, was it yesterday
We heard the sweet bells over the bay?
In the caverns where we lay,
Through the surf and through the swell,
The far-off sound of a silver bell?
Sand-strewn caverns, cool and deep,
Where the winds are all asleep;
Where the spent lights quiver and gleam,
Where the salt weed sways in the stream,
Where the sea beasts, ranged all round,
Feed in the ooze of their pasture ground;
Where the sea snakes coil and twine,
Dry their mail and bask in the brine;
Where great whales come sailing by,
Sail and sail, with unshut eye,
Round the world for ever and aye?
    When did music come this way?
    Children dear, was it yesterday?

Children dear, was it yesterday
(Call yet once) that she went away?
Once she sate with you and me,
On a red gold throne in the heart of the sea,
And the youngest sate on her knee.
She combed its bright hair, and she tended it well,
When down swung the sound of a far-off bell.
She sighed, she looked up through the clear green sea;
She said: "I must go, for my kinsfolk pray
In the little gray church on the shore today.
'Twill be Easter-time in the world — ah me!
And I lose my poor soul, Merman, here with thee."
I said: "Go up, dear heart, through the waves;
Say thy prayer, and come back to the kind sea-caves!"
She smiled, she went up through the surf in the bay.
     Children dear, was it yesterday?

Children dear, were we long alone?
"The sea grows stormy, the little ones moan.
Long prayers," I said, "in the world they say.
Come!" I said; and we rose through the surf in the bay.
We went up the beach, by the sandy down
Where the sea-stocks bloom, to the white-walled town.
Through the narrow paved streets, where all was still,
To the little gray church on the windy hill.
From the church came a murmur of folk at their prayers,
But we stood without in the cold blowing airs.
We climbed on the graves, on the stones worn with rains,
And we gazed up the aisle through the small leaded panes.
     She sate by the pillar; we saw her clear:
     "Margaret, hist! come quick, we are here!
     Dear heart," I said, "we are long alone;
     The sea grows stormy, the little ones moan."

But, ah, she gave me never a look,
For her eyes were sealed to the holy book!
    Loud prays the priest; shut stands the **door.**
    Come away, children, call no more!
    Come away, come down, call no **more!**

    Down, down, down!
    Down to the depths of the sea!
She sits at her wheel in the humming **town,**
    Singing most joyfully.
Hark what she sings: "O joy, O joy,
For the humming street, and the child with its **toy!**
For the priest, and the, bell, and the holy well;
    For the wheel where I spun,
    And the blessed light of the sun!"
    And so she sings her fill,
    Singing most joyfully,
    Till the spindle drops from her hand,
    And the whizzing wheel stands still.
She steals to the window, and looks at the **sand,**
    And over the sand at the sea;
    And her eyes are set in a stare;
    And anon there breaks a sigh,
    And anon there drops a tear,
    From a sorrow-clouded eye,
    And a heart sorrow-laden,
    A long, long sigh
For the cold strange eyes of a little **Mermaiden,**
And the gleam of her golden hair.

    Come away, away, children;
    Come, children, come down!
    The hoarse wind blows colder;
    Lights shine in the town.

She will start from her slumber
When gusts shake the door;
She will hear the winds howling,
Will hear the waves roar.
We shall see, while above us
The waves roar and whirl,
A ceiling of amber,
A pavement of pearl.
Singing: "Here came a mortal,
But faithless was she!
And alone dwell for ever
The kings of the sea."

But, children, at midnight,
When soft the winds blow,
When clear falls the moonlight,
When spring tides are low;
When sweet airs come seaward
From heaths starred with broom,
And high rocks throw mildly
On the blanched sands a gloom;
Up the still, glistening beaches,
Up the creeks we will hie,
Over banks of bright seaweed
The ebb tide leaves dry.
We will gaze, from the sand hills,
At the white, sleeping town;
At the church on the hillside —
And then come back down.
Singing: "There dwells a loved one,
But cruel is she!
She left lonely for ever
The kings of the sea."

Silver

WALTER DE LA MARE

You will seldom look again upon a countryside drenched in moonlight without finding it more beautiful because of the poet's silver etching.

Slowly, silently, now the moon
Walks the night in her silver shoon;
This way, and that, she peers, and sees
Silver fruit upon silver trees;
One by one the casements catch
Her beams beneath the silvery thatch;
Couched in his kennel, like a log,
With paws of silver sleeps the dog;
From their shadowy cote the white breasts peep
Of doves in a silver-feathered sleep;
A harvest mouse goes scampering by,
With silver claws, and silver eye;
And moveless fish in the water gleam,
By silver reeds in a silver stream.

XI: Figurative Language

Even in ordinary conversation, plain speech will not always express one's entire meaning; or rather, the "plainest" language is often not plain at all, but decorated with comparisons and figures.

In plain speech, "The brothers look very much alike"; in figurative, "They are as like as two pennies." Which is the more effective statement? — The second, of course.

Many figures of speech are so commonly used that they pass unnoticed: a face like a thundercloud; skies like lead; like as two peas; light as a feather; slow as molasses in January; clock-like regularity; moonface; butter-fingers; catcalls. Like old coins, some are so worn that they have almost lost their identity. Once, however, they were fresh and new.

Often a comparison enables one to visualize something he has never seen. By means of comparisons, a traveler in China shows us a walled village seen from a hilltop — "Here lay spread out the city wall filled with a sea of blue-back tiled roofs" — and he describes long files of marching pilgrims, "winding like endless snakes along the narrow stone trail."

The two most frequent figures of speech are similes and metaphors. A *simile* expresses a comparison by using some such word as *like* or *as:* He is as gaunt as a scarecrow . . . She had eyes like a frog . . . The tall stacks, "like giant pencils, write broad smears" against the sky.

A *metaphor* does not use words of comparison. It makes a figurative statement as if it were literally true: He is a scarecrow . . . She had frog's eyes. Because of its directness of statement, metaphorical language has great force and vigor: She'll make him eat his words! . . . His rage burst forth in a mighty flame.

Names are often metaphorical. They suggest a picturesque image in a single phrase or word: Needle Mountain; City of the Golden Gate; Hungry Hollow; skyscraper; cow-puncher; buttercup; goldenrod.

People enjoy seeing resemblances, whether between beautiful objects, such as great white clouds and white-winged ships, or between less beautiful things, such as a pepper pot and a hot-tempered child.

The ability to discover resemblances is poetic. To some degree, everyone shares this power, even very young children. The small boy who said that Vichy water tasted as if his foot were asleep made a fresh and vivid comparison. Before him, probably nobody had noticed the likeness between the tingling taste of the mineral water and the tingling sensation which pricks a foot that has gone to sleep.

A third figure of speech is called *personification*. Everyone tends to personify some things. The little girl attributes life and feeling to her doll. The little boy half-way believes his wooden horse understands him when he speaks to it. The moon, everybody knows, is a woman. Ships and engines are feminine (perhaps because they are sometimes so perverse!); the great sun is masculine.

Often the winter wind races through the night as if it were alive. In certain moods, all outdoor nature seems to sympathize with us, sharing our trouble or gladness.

> The winds come to me from the fields of sleep,
>   And all the earth is gay;
>   Land and sea
>   Give themselves up to jollity,
>   And with the heart of May
>   Doth every beast keep holiday.

Figurative language is interesting and colorful. It abounds in pictures. These pictures are pleasing both in themselves and because of their power to call up other interesting or beautiful images. For all words have a twofold power. First, they have a definite meaning. Second, in addition to their meaning, they have the power of suggesting ideas and images which are associated with the words, though not actually a part of the meaning.

The word *mouse* names a small, grayish-brown rodent. What does it suggest? — Oh, a variety of things! A fat tabby keeping watch at a keyhole; cheese and traps; girls squealing with fright; a gnawing sound in the wainscoting in the dead of night.

Some words are especially rich in suggestion; *harbor*, for instance, and *pilgrim* and *knight*. What romance, what adventure, what far places they suggest! And how they set one's imagination astir! Some words seem to come "trailing clouds of glory" in their wake. *Star* is such a one. Poets never tire of its beauty, discovering therein always some new splendor. Longfellow, you remember, called the stars "the forgetmenots of the angels." Shakespeare, seeing them grow dim with the coming dawn, said,

> Night's candles are burnt out, and jocund day
> Stands tiptoe on the misty mountain tops.

Another poet, speeding over the darkened earth in a railway train, saw them thus:

> All the beautiful stars of the sky,
>   The silver doves of the forest of Night,
> Over the dull earth swarm and fly,
>   Companions of our flight.

The poet weaves figures of beauty into the pattern of his verse, as if it were some rich silken tapestry.

In the Train

James Thomson

Had you realized how swift and beautiful is the flight of a train?

As we rush, as we rush in the Train,
  The trees and the houses go wheeling back,
But the starry heavens above the plain
  Come flying on our track.

All the beautiful stars of the sky,
  The silver doves of the forest of Night,
Over the dull earth swarm and fly,
  Companions of our flight.

We will rush ever on without fear;
  Let the goal be far, the flight be fleet!
For we carry the Heavens with us, dear,
  While the Earth slips from our feet!

Dream Pedlary

THOMAS LOVELL BEDDOES

These dream metaphors are as delicate as rose petals.

If there were dreams to sell,
 What would you buy?
Some cost a passing bell;
 Some a light sigh,
That shakes from Life's fresh crown
Only a rose leaf down.
If there were dreams to sell,
Merry and sad to tell,
And the crier rang the bell,
 What would you buy?

A cottage lone and still,
 With bowers nigh,
Shadowy, my woes to still,
 Until I die.
Such pearl from Life's fresh crown
Fain would I shake me down.
Were dreams to have at will,
This would best heal my ill,
 This would I buy.

Forbearance

Ralph Waldo Emerson

The poet clothes a moral truth in beautiful imagery. As in many of the finest poems, the meaning lies too deep to be grasped at a single reading.

The two poems on this page are similar in meaning, but how different is the figurative language in which the meanings are expressed!

Hast thou named all the birds without a gun?
Loved the wood-rose, and left it on its stalk?
At rich men's tables eaten bread and pulse?
Unarmed, faced danger with a heart of trust?
And loved so well a high behavior,
In man or maid, that thou from speech refrained,
Nobility more nobly to repay?
O, be my friend, and teach me to be thine!

Forbearance

Edward Robert Bulwer-Lytton

Close not thy hand upon the innocent joy
    That trusts itself within thy reach.   It may,
Or may not, linger.   Thou canst but destroy
    The wingéd wanderer.   Let it go or stay.
Love thou the rose, yet leave it on its stem.
        Think!   Midas starved by turning all to gold.
        Blessed are those that spare, and that withhold;
Because the whole world shall be trusted them.

The Book

WILLIAM DRUMMOND

What infinite variety in the pictures of this Book! And what different stories its chapters tell!

Of this fair volume which we World do name,
If we the sheets and leaves could turn with care,
Of Him who it corrects and did it frame,
We clear might read the art and wisdom rare;

Find out His power, which wildest powers doth tame,
His providence extending everywhere,
His justice, which proud rebels doth not spare,
In every page, no period of the same.

But silly we, like foolish children, rest
Well pleased with colored vellum, leaves of gold,
Fair dangling ribbands, leaving what is best,
On the great Writer's sense ne'er taking hold;
Or if by chance we stay our minds on aught,
It is some picture on the margin wrought.

Bill and Joe

OLIVER WENDELL HOLMES

Are you not surprised to see how much of figurative language this plain, simple talk contains?

Come, dear old comrade, you and I
Will steal an hour from days gone by,
The shining days when life was new,
And all was bright with morning dew,
The lusty days of long ago,
When you were Bill and I was Joe.

Your name may flaunt a titled trail
Proud as a cockerel's rainbow tail,
And mine as brief appendix wear
As Tam O'Shanter's luckless mare;
Today, old friend, remember still
That I am Joe and you are Bill.

You've won the great world's envied prize,
And grand you look in people's eyes,
With H O N. and LL. D.
In big brave letters, fair to see, —
Your fist, old fellow! off they go! —
How are you, Bill?   How are you, Joe?

You've worn the judge's ermined robe;
You've taught your name to half the globe;
You've sung mankind a deathless strain;
You've made the dead past live again:
The world may call you what it will,
But you and I are Joe and Bill.

The chaffing young folks stare and say,
"See those old buffers, bent and gray, —
They talk like fellows in their teens!
Mad, poor old boys! That's what it means," —
And shake their heads; they little know
The throbbing hearts of Bill and Joe! —

How Bill forgets his hour of pride,
While Joe sits smiling at his side;
How Joe, in spite of time's disguise
Finds the old schoolmate in his eyes, —
Those calm, stern eyes that melt and fill
As Joe looks fondly up at Bill.

Ah, pensive scholar, what is fame?
A fitful tongue of leaping flame;
A giddy whirlwind's fickle gust,
That lifts a pinch of mortal dust;
A few swift years, and who can show
Which dust was Bill and which was Joe?

The weary idol takes his stand,
Holds out his bruised and aching hand,
While gaping thousands come and go, —
How vain it seems, this empty show!
Till all at once his pulses thrill; —
'Tis poor old Joe's "God bless you, Bill!"

And shall we breathe in happier spheres
The names that pleased our mortal ears;
In some sweet lull of harp and song,
For earth-born spirits none too long,
Just whispering of the world below
Where this was Bill and that was Joe?

No matter; while our home is here
No sounding name is half so dear;
When fades at length our lingering day,
Who cares what pompous tombstones say?
Read on the hearts that love us still,
Hic jacet Joe.   *Hic jacet* Bill.

The Latin expression *Hic jacet* means "Here lies."

Autumn

THOMAS HOOD

*A lonely, silent figure is Autumn as he stands in the misty dawn, his crown
of golden corn pearled with dewy cobwebs.*

I saw old Autumn in the misty morn
Stand shadowless like Silence, listening
To silence, for no lonely bird would sing
Into his hollow ear from woods forlorn,
Nor lowly hedge nor solitary thorn; —
Shaking his languid locks all dewy bright
With tangled gossamer that fell by night,
Pearling his coronet of golden corn.

Frost Tonight

Edith M. Thomas

These lines are memorable for their clearness of picture as well as for their thought and feeling.

Apple-green west and an orange bar,
And the crystal eye of a lone, one star . . .
And "Child, take the shears and cut what you will;
Frost tonight — so clear and dead-still."

Then I sally forth, half sad, half proud,
And I come to the velvet, imperial crowd,
The wine-red, the gold, the crimson, the pied, —
The dahlias that reign by the garden-side.

The dahlias I might not touch till tonight!
A gleam of the shears in the fading light,
And I gathered them all — the splendid throng,
And in one great sheaf I bore them along.

In my garden of Life with its all-late flowers
I heed a Voice in the shrinking hours:
"Frost tonight — so clear and dead-still . . ."
Half sad, half proud, my arms I fill.

The Chambered Nautilus

OLIVER WENDELL HOLMES

The beauty of its pictures and the nobility of its aspiration have made this a favorite poem of the American people.

This is the ship of pearl, which, poets feign,
   Sails the unshadowed main, —
   The venturous bark that flings
On the sweet summer wind its purpled wings
In gulfs enchanted, where the Siren sings,
   And coral reefs lie bare,
Where the cold sea-maids rise to sun their streaming hair.

Its webs of living gauze no more unfurl;
   Wrecked is the ship of pearl!
   And every chambered cell,
Where its dim dreaming life was wont to dwell,
As the frail tenant shaped his growing shell,
   Before thee lies revealed, —
Its irised ceiling rent, its sunless crypt unsealed.

Year after year beheld the silent toil
   That spread his lustrous coil;
   Still, as the spiral grew,
He left the past year's dwelling for the new,
Stole with soft step its shining archway through,
   Built up its idle door,
Stretched in his last-found home, and knew the old no
       more.

Thanks for the heavenly message brought by thee,
   Child of the wandering sea,
   Cast from her lap, forlorn!
From thy dead lips a clearer note is born
Than ever Triton blew from wreathéd horn!
   While on mine ear it rings,
Through the deep caves of thought I hear a voice that
       sings: —

Build thee more stately mansions, O my soul,
   As the swift seasons roll!
   Leave thy low-vaulted past!
Let each new temple, nobler than the last,
Shut thee from heaven with a dome more vast,
   Till thou at length art free,
Leaving thine outgrown shell by life's unresting sea.

Invictus

William Ernest Henley

"Invictus" is the Latin word for "unconquered." No matter how over-whelming the odds in the battle of life, or how dark the threat of Death, the courageous spirit does not blench nor yield.

Out of the night that covers me,
  Black as the Pit from pole to pole,
I thank whatever gods may be
  For my unconquerable soul.

In the fell clutch of circumstance
  I have not winced nor cried aloud.
Under the bludgeonings of chance
  My head is bloody, but unbowed.

Beyond this place of wrath and tears
  Looms but the Horror of the shade,
And yet the menace of the years
  Finds and shall find me unafraid.

It matters not how strait the gate,
  How charged with punishments the scroll,
I am the master of my fate:
  I am the captain of my soul.

In Flanders Fields

John McCrae

This poem, written by a Canadian army surgeon, suggests the reason why poppies are worn on Memorial Day in memory of the men who died in the World War. Notice that there is no hatred here; only beauty and longing that the torch of truth shall be held high. The poet speaks for all people who believe their cause to be just.

In Flanders fields the poppies blow
Between the crosses, row on row,
    That mark our place; and in the sky
    The larks, still bravely singing, fly
Scarce heard amid the guns below.

We are the Dead.   Short days ago
We lived, felt dawn, saw sunset glow,
    Loved and were loved, and now we lie
    In Flanders fields.

Take up our quarrel with the foe:
To you from failing hands we throw
    The torch; be yours to hold it high.
    If ye break faith with us who die
We shall not sleep, though poppies grow
    In Flanders fields.

The Night-Piece: To Julia

ROBERT HERRICK

After three hundred years the metaphors of this poem still keep their quaint and shining luster.

Her eyes the glowworm lend thee,
The shooting stars attend thee;
    And the elves also,
    Whose little eyes glow
Like the sparks of fire, befriend thee.

No Will-o'-the-wisp mislight thee,
Nor snake or slow-worm bite thee;
    But on, on thy way
    Not making a stay,
Since ghost there's none to affright thee.

Let not the dark thee cumber:
What though the moon does slumber?
    The stars of the night
    Will lend thee their light
Like tapers clear without number.

Rose's Red

Even the unlettered boy in the plantation cabin turns to figurative language to tell his love. For all they are worn and homely, the comparisons give real pleasure.

Rose's red, vi'let's blue,
Sugar is sweet — but not lak you.
De vi'lets fade, de roses fall;
But you gets sweeter, all in all.

As shore as de grass grows 'round de stump,
You is my darlin' Sugar Lump.
W'en de sun don't shine de day is cold,
But my love fer you do not git old.

De ocean's deep, de sky is blue,
Sugar is sweet, an' so is you:
De ocean waves an' de sky gits pale,
But my love are true, an' it never fail.

CABIN LOVE RHYME

Be True

WILLIAM SHAKESPEARE

In this quotation there is only one simile, and that a very simple one. Does it add anything to the meaning? The lines are from "Hamlet."

This above all: to thine own self be true;
And it must follow, as the night the day,
Thou canst not then be false to any man.

To Althea, from Prison

RICHARD LOVELACE

Imprisoned by stone walls and iron bars, the courtier poet yet found freedom.

Stone walls do not a prison make,
  Nor iron bars a cage;
Minds innocent and quiet take
  That for a hermitage;
If I have freedom in my love
  And in my soul am free,
Angels alone, that soar above,
  Enjoy such liberty.

To the Grasshopper and the Cricket

Leigh Hunt

As you read, doesn't your heart catch at the feel of June, and beat more happily at the sound of the cricket nicking the moments as they pass?

Green little vaulter in the sunny grass,
Catching your heart up at the feel of June,
Sole voice that's heard amidst the lazy noon,
When even the bees lag at the summoning brass;

And you, warm little housekeeper, who class
With those who think the candles come too soon,
Loving the fire, and with your tricksome tune
Nick the glad silent moments as they pass;

O sweet and tiny cousins, that belong,
One to the fields, the other to the hearth,
Both have your sunshine; both, though small, are
    strong
At your clear hearts; and both seem given to earth
To sing in thoughtful ears their natural song —
In doors and out, summer and winter, Mirth.

THE·LITTLE·HORSE·MUST·THINK·IT·QUEER
TO·STOP·WITHOUT·A·FARMHOUSE·NEAR

XII: THE KINDS OF POETRY

Poetry is of different kinds. Narrative verse tells a story. Lyric verse is written to express an emotion or a mood. Dramatic verse, as the name implies, takes the form of dramatic dialogue. There are no hard and fast lines separating the different types. Indeed, it is often difficult, if not impossible, to decide whether the poet is interested chiefly in the story he tells or in the emotion it conveys. Nor does it greatly matter, though the reader can better appreciate the poem if he understands the poet's purpose.

A very long narrative dealing with lofty subjects is called an epic. Milton's *Paradise Lost* is an epic, and so are the *Odyssey* and the *Iliad*. Most people consider *Evangeline* and *The Courtship of Miles Standish* somewhat too slight to be real epics. Some narrative poems are very short. "Little Giffin" is one of these. Many of the old ballads are narratives although they were originally intended to be sung. "The Highwayman" is a stirring modern ballad.

In the beginning, all poetry was sung or chanted. Because the song was often accompanied by the lyre (a U-shaped stringed instrument of ancient Greece), the word "lyric" came to be applied to all poems suitable for singing. In the modern song, verse and music still accompany each other.

Lyric poems are written to express a feeling. The poet may be saddened by the sight of leafless winter trees,

> Bare ruined choirs, where late the sweet birds sang.

Or he may rejoice at seeing his country's flag pass by,

> A bit of bunting, but how it gleams,
> Fashioned of valor and woven of dreams.

[273]

A cloud, a flower, a battle bravely fought, a little child at play — whatever stirs the emotions may be the occasion for a poem.

Certain types of lyrics have special names. A poem of lamentation for the dead is called an elegy. An ode is a poem of praise, usually dignified in tone and varied in metrical pattern. Sonnets are a lyric form also.

Some of the most beautiful poetry in the world is in the form of drama. Shakespeare's plays are all written in verse, except for occasional short passages in prose.

Humorous verse, or light verse as it is known, has beguiled many a tedious hour into smiling. Even the most disgruntled boredom must yield to amusement at the discontented sugar broker.

> A gentleman of City fame
>   Now claims your kind attention;
> West India broking was his game,
>   His name I shall not mention;
>   No one of finely pointed sense
>   Would violate a confidence,
>   And shall *I* go
>   And do it?   No.
>   His name I shall not mention.

The Solitary Reaper

WILLIAM WORDSWORTH

This descriptive lyric has long been a favorite of English-speaking peoples. Beautiful though it is in sound and picture, it seems always to suggest things even more hauntingly beautiful, too vague and far to be put into words. Two lines in particular have an almost magic power of suggestion:

> *"old, unhappy, far-off things,*
> *And battles long ago."*

Behold her, single in the field,
Yon solitary Highland Lass!
Reaping and singing by herself;
Stop here, or gently pass!
Alone she cuts and binds the grain,
And sings a melancholy strain;
O listen! for the vale profound
Is overflowing with the sound.

No nightingale did ever chaunt
More welcome notes to weary bands
Of travelers in some shady haunt,
Among Arabian sands:
A voice so thrilling ne'er was heard
In springtime from the cuckoo bird,
Breaking the silence of the seas
Among the farthest Hebrides.

Will no one tell me what she sings? —
Perhaps the plaintive numbers flow
For old, unhappy, far-off things,
And battles long ago;

[275]

Or is it some more humble lay,
Familiar matter of today?
Some natural sorrow, loss, or pain,
That has been, and may be again?

Whate'er the theme, the maiden sang
As if her song could have no ending;
I saw her singing at her work,
And o'er the sickle bending; —
I listened, motionless and still;
And as I mounted up the hill,
The music in my heart I bore
Long after it was heard no more.

Stopping by Woods on a Snowy Evening

ROBERT FROST

The very essence of New England winter is caught in this brief description.

Whose woods these are I think I know.
His house is in the village though;
He will not see me stopping here
To watch his woods fill up with snow.

The little horse must think it queer
To stop without a farmhouse near
Between the woods and frozen lake
The darkest evening of the year.

He gives his harness bells a shake
To ask if there is some mistake.
The only other sound's the sweep
Of easy wind and downy flake.

The woods are lovely, dark and deep.
But I have promises to keep,
And miles to go before I sleep,
And miles to go before I sleep.

The Inevitable

SARAH KNOWLES BOLTON

This lyric is what is known as didactic verse, because it teaches a lesson.

I like the man who faces what he must
With step triumphant and a heart of cheer;
Who fights the daily battle without fear;
Sees his hopes fail, yet keeps unfaltering trust
That God is God, — that somehow, true and just
His plans work out for mortals; not a tear
Is shed when fortune, which the world holds dear,
Falls from his grasp — better, with love, a crust
Than living in dishonor; envies not,
Nor loses faith in man; but does his best,
Nor ever murmurs at his humbler lot;
But with a smile and words of hope, gives zest
To every toiler. He alone is great
Who by a life heroic conquers fate.

Give All to Love

RALPH WALDO EMERSON

This lyric also is didactic. Do you like its picturesque phrasing less or more than the simpler statement of "The Inevitable"?

Give all to love;
Obey thy heart;
Friends, kindred, days,
Estate, good fame,
Plans, credit, and the Muse —
Nothing refuse.

'Tis a brave master;
Let it have scope:
Follow it utterly,
Hope beyond hope:
High and more high
It dives into noon,
With wing unspent,
Untold intent;
But it is a god,
Knows its own path
And the outlets of the sky.

It was never for the mean;
It requireth courage stout;
Souls above doubt,
Valor unbending,
It will reward; —
They shall return
More than they were,
And ever ascending.

Song

THOMAS LOVELL BEDDOES

This Song is cherished, not for any lesson, but for sheer loveliness.

How many times do I love thee, dear?
   Tell me how many thoughts there be
      In the atmosphere
      Of a new-fallen year,
Whose white and sable hours appear
   The latest flake of Eternity:
So many times do I love thee, dear.

How many times do I love again?
   Tell me how many beads there are
      In a silver chain
      Of evening rain,
Unraveled from the tumbling main,
   And threading the eye of a yellow star:
So many times do I love again.

Up-Hill

Christina Rossetti

Would this lyric lend itself to musical accompaniment as well as Beddoes' Song would?

Does the road wind up-hill all the way?
  Yes, to the very end.
Will the day's journey take the whole long day?
  From morn to night, my friend.

But is there for the night a resting-place?
  A roof for when the slow, dark hours begin.
May not the darkness hide it from my face?
  You cannot miss that inn.

Shall I meet other wayfarers at night?
  Those who have gone before.
Then must I knock or call when just in sight?
  They will not keep you waiting at that door.

Shall I find comfort, travel-sore and weak?
  Of labor you shall find the sum.
Will there be beds for me and all who seek?
  Yea, beds for all who come.

An Old Dog

Celia Duffin

The old dog's love for his master finds voice in this quiet lyric.

Now that no shrill hunting horn
Can arouse me at the morn,
Deaf I lie the long day through
Dreaming firelight dreams of you.
Waiting patient through it all
Till the greater huntsman call.

If we are, as people say,
But the creatures of a day,
Let me live, when we must part,
A little longer in your heart.
You were all the God I knew,
I was faithful unto you.

Father William

LEWIS CARROLL

How much duller the world would have been without Lewis Carroll's nonsense verse!

You are old, Father William," the young man said,
 "And your hair has become very white;
And yet you incessantly stand on your head —
 Do you think, at your age, it is right?"

"In my youth," Father William replied to his son,
 "I feared it might injure the brain;
But now that I'm perfectly sure I have none,
 Why, I do it again and again."

"You are old," said the youth, "as I mentioned before,
 And have grown most uncommonly fat;
Yet you turned a back-somersault in at the door —
 Pray, what is the reason of that?"

"In my youth," said the sage, as he shook his gray locks,
 "I kept all my limbs very supple
By the use of this ointment — one shilling the box —
 Allow me to sell you a couple?"

"You are old," said the youth, "and your jaws are too weak
 For anything tougher than suet;
Yet you finished the goose, with the bones and the beak —
 Pray, how did you manage to do it?"

"In my youth," said his father, "I took to the law
    And argued each case with my wife;
And the muscular strength which it gave to my jaw,
    Has lasted the rest of my life."

"You are old," said the youth, "one would hardly suppose
    That your eye was as steady as ever;
Yet you balanced an eel on the end of your nose —
    What made you so awfully clever?"

"I have answered three questions, and that is enough,"
    Said his father; "don't give yourself airs!
Do you think I can listen all day to such stuff?
    Be off, or I'll kick you downstairs!"

Jonathan Bing

B. Curtis Brown

Poor Jonathan!   Do you suppose he dreamed it?

Poor old Jonathan Bing
Went out in his carriage to visit the King,
But everyone pointed and said, "Look at that!
Jonathan Bing has forgotten his hat!"
(He'd forgotten his hat!)

Poor old Jonathan Bing
Went home and put on a new hat for the King,
But up by the palace a soldier said, "Hi!
You can't see the King; you've forgotten your tie!"
(He'd forgotten his tie!)

Poor old Jonathan Bing,
He put on a beautiful tie for the King,
But when he arrived an Archbishop said, "Ho!
You can't come to court in pajamas, you know!"

Poor old Jonathan Bing
Went home and addressed a short note to the King:
"If you please will excuse me I won't come to tea,
For home's the best place for all people like me!"

The Dirty Old Man

WILLIAM ALLINGHAM

Do old, tumble-down houses interest you? Here is one which stands as plain to view today in a narrative poem as ever it stood in brick and wood on a London street of long ago.

In a dirty old house lived a Dirty Old Man;
Soap, towels, or brushes were not in his plan.
For forty long years, as the neighbors declared,
His house never once had been cleaned or repaired.

'Twas a scandal and shame to the businesslike street,
One terrible blot in a ledger so neat:
The shop full of hardware, but black as a hearse,
And the rest of the mansion a thousand times worse.

Outside, the old plaster, all spatter and stain,
Looked spotty in sunshine and streaky in rain;
The windowsills sprouted with mildewy grass,
And the panes, from being broken, were known to be glass.

On the rickety signboard no learning could spell
The merchant who sold, or the goods he'd to sell;
But for house and for man a new title took growth,
Like a fungus, — the Dirt gave its name to them both.

Within, there were carpets and cushions of dust,
The wood was half rot, and the metal half rust,
Old curtains — half cobwebs — hung grimly aloof;
'Twas a Spiders' Elysium from cellar to roof.

There, king of the spiders, the Dirty Old Man
Lives busy and dirty as ever he can;
With dirt on his fingers and dirt on his face,
For the Dirty Old Man thinks the dirt no disgrace.

From his wig to his shoes, from his coat to his shirt,
His clothes are a proverb, a marvel of dirt;
The dirt is pervading, unfading, exceeding, —
Yet the Dirty Old Man has both learning and breeding.

Fine dames from their carriages, noble and fair,
Have entered his shop — less to buy than to stare;
And have afterwards said, though the dirt was so frightful,
The Dirty Man's manners were truly delightful.

They pried not upstairs, through the dirt and the gloom,
Nor peeped at the door of the wonderful room
That gossips made much of, in accents subdued,
But whose inside no mortal might boast to have viewed.

That room — forty years since, folk settled and decked it.
The luncheon's prepared, and the guests are expected.
The handsome young host he is gallant and gay,
For his love and her friends will be with him today.

With solid and dainty the table is drest,
The wine beams its brightest, the flowers bloom their best;
Yet the host need not smile, and no guests will appear,
For his sweetheart is dead, as he shortly shall hear.

Full forty years since, turned the key in that door.
'Tis a room deaf and dumb 'mid the city's uproar.
The guests, for whose joyance that table was spread,
May now enter as ghosts, for they're every one dead.

Through a chink in the shutter dim lights come and go;
The seats are in order, the dishes a-row;
But the luncheon was wealth to the rat and the mouse
Whose descendants have long left the Dirty Old House.

Cup and platter are masked in thick layers of dust;
The flowers fallen to powder, the wine swathed in crust;
A nosegay was laid before one special chair,
And the faded blue ribbon that bound it lies there.

The old man has played out his parts in the scene.
Wherever he now is, I hope he's more clean.
Yet give we a thought free of scoffing or ban
To that Dirty Old House and that Dirty Old Man.

In explanation of this poem, Allingham wrote: "A singular man, named Nathaniel Bentley, for many years kept a large hardware shop in Leaden-hall Street, London. He was best known as Dirty Dick (Dick, for alliteration's sake, probably), and his place of business as the Dirty Warehouse. He died about the year 1809. These verses accord with the accounts respecting himself and his house."

Latter Day Warnings

OLIVER WENDELL HOLMES

A Mr. Miller and a Mr. Cummings proclaimed in sermons that the world was coming to an end.   Whose opinion on the matter seems to you the more shrewd, theirs or the poet's?

When legislators keep the law,
   When banks dispense with bolts and locks,
When berries — whortle, rasp, and straw —
   Grow bigger *downwards* through the box, —

When he that selleth house or land
   Shows leak in roof or flaw in right,
When haberdashers choose the stand
   Whose window hath the broadest light, —

When preachers tell us all they think,
   And party leaders all they mean,
When what we pay for, that we drink,
   From real grape and coffee-bean, —

When lawyers take what they would give,
   And doctors give what they would take,
When city fathers eat to live,
   Save when they fast for conscience' sake, —

When one that hath a horse on sale
   Shall bring his merit to the proof,
Without a lie for every nail
   That holds the iron on the hoof, —

When in the usual place for rips
    Our gloves are stitched with special care,
And guarded well the whalebone tips
    Where first umbrellas need repair, —

Till then let Cummings blaze away,
    And Miller's saints blow up the globe;
But when you see that blessed day,
    Then order your ascension robe!

A Discontented Sugar Broker

W. S. GILBERT

These stanzas cut almost as many amusing capers in rhyme and rhythm on the page as the fat sugar broker cut on the streets of London.

A gentleman of City fame
    Now claims your kind attention;
West India broking was his game,
    His name I shall not mention;
      No one of finely pointed sense
      Would violate a confidence,
        And shall *I* go
        And do it? No.
His name I shall not mention.

He had a trusty wife and true,
    And very cosy quarters,
A manager, a boy or two,
    Six clerks, and seven porters.

A broker must be doing well
(As any lunatic can tell)
    Who can employ
    An active boy,
Six clerks, and seven porters.

His knocker advertised no dun,
    No losses made him sulky,
He had one sorrow — only one —
    He was extremely bulky.
        A man must be, I beg to state,
        Exceptionally fortunate
            Who owns his chief
            And only grief
Is being very bulky.

"This load," he'd say, "I cannot bear,
    I'm nineteen stone or twenty!
Henceforward I'll go in for air
    And exercise in plenty."
        Most people think that, should it come,
        They can reduce a bulging tum
            To measures fair
            By taking air
And exercise in plenty.

In every weather, every day,
    Dry, muddy, wet, or gritty,
He took to dancing all the way
    From Brompton to the City.
        You do not often get the chance
        Of seeing sugar brokers dance
            From their abode
            In Fulham Road
Through Brompton to the City.

He braved the gay and guileless laugh
   Of children with their nusses,
The loud uneducated chaff
   Of clerks on omnibuses.
     Against all minor things that rack
     A nicely balanced mind, I'll back
      The noisy chaff
      And ill-bred laugh
   Of clerks on omnibuses.

His friends, who heard his money chink,
   And saw the house he rented,
And knew his wife, could never think
   What made him discontented.
     It never struck their simple minds
     That fads are of eccentric kinds,
      Nor would they own
      That fat alone
   Could make him discontented.

"Your riches know no kind of pause,
   Your trade is fast advancing,
You dance — but not for joy, because
   You weep as you are dancing.
     To dance implies that man is glad,
     To weep implies that man is sad,
      But here are you
      Who do the two —
   You weep as you are dancing!"

His mania soon got noised about
   And into all the papers —
His size increased beyond a doubt
   For all his reckless capers:

It may seem singular to you,
But all his friends admit it true —
   The more he found
   His figure round,
The more he cut his capers.

His bulk increased — no matter that —
He tried the more to toss it —
He never spoke of it as "fat"
   But "adipose deposit."
     Upon my word, it seems to me
     Unpardonable vanity
      (And worse than that)
      To call your fat
An "adipose deposit."

At length his brawny knees gave way,
   And on the carpet sinking,
Upon his shapeless back he lay
   And kicked away like winking.
     Instead of seeing in his state
     The finger of unswerving Fate,
      He labored still
      To work his will,
   And kicked away like winking.

His friends, disgusted with him now,
   Away in silence wended —
I hardly like to tell you how
   This dreadful story ended.
     The shocking sequel to impart,
     I must employ the limner's art —
      If you would know,
      This sketch will show
How his exertions ended.

I hate to preach — I hate to prate —
I'm no fanatic croaker,
But learn contentment from the fate
Of this West India broker.
He'd everything a man of taste
Could ever want, except a waist:
And discontent
His size anent,
And bootless perseverance blind,
Completely wrecked the peace of mind
Of this West India broker.

The Bell-Man

ROBERT HERRICK

No doubt Herrick was awakened many a time, three hundred years ago, by the sound of the bell-man's voice, calling the hour of night. You may be sure that the night watchman's song had not much variety of tune.

From noise of Scare-fires rest ye free,
From Murders — Benedicite.
From all mischances, that may fright
Your pleasing slumbers in the night:
Mercie secure ye all, and keep
The Goblin from ye, while ye sleep.
Past one a-clock, and almost two,
My Masters all, *Good day to you!*

Benedicite (pronounced běn'ē-dĭs'ĭ-tě) here means "May you be delivered."

Overheard on a Saltmarsh

Harold Monro

*Can you picture the shadowy figures of the speakers in this dramatic
dialogue? And can you see, in the greenish-white light of the moon, the
eerie elfin scene?*

Nymph, nymph, what are your beads?

Green glass, goblin.   Why do you stare at them?
Give them me.
                     No.
Give them me.   Give them me.
                              No.
Then I will howl all night in the reeds,
Lie in the mud and howl for them.

Goblin, why do you love them so?

They are better than stars or water,
Better than voices of winds that sing,
Better than any man's fair daughter,
Your green glass beads on a silver ring.

Hush, I stole them out of the moon.

Give me your beads, I want them.
                              No.
I will howl in the deep lagoon
For your green glass beads, I love them so.
Give them me.   Give them.
                     No.

The Conclusion

Even such is Time, that takes in trust
　　Our youth, our joys, our all we have,
And pays us but with earth and dust;
　　Who in the dark and silent grave,
When we have wandered all our ways,
Shuts up the story of our days;
　　But from this earth, this grave, this dust,
My God shall raise me up, I trust.

An epitaph is an inscription for a tomb. English literature has preserved many such short, noble stanzas. This one was written by the same Sir Walter Raleigh who named Virginia in honor of the Virgin Queen.

The following lines were cut on the gravestone of Edward Courtenay, Earl of Devonshire.

On a Gravestone

What I gave, I have;
What I spent, I had;
What I kept, I lost.

Epitaph

In Obitum M. S.   X Maij, 1614

May! Be thou never graced with birds that sing,
　　Nor Flora's pride!
In thee all flowers and roses spring,
　　Mine only died.

The Latin words under the title mean "On the Death of M. S. May 10, 1614. *Flora* is the goddess of flowers. In spring, when flowers waken from the long winter sleep, the death of a child seems especially sad. This epitaph was written by William Browne.

Lift Up Your Heads, O Ye Gates!

The Twenty-fourth Psalm, from the Bible, is really an ode of praise.

The earth is the Lord's, and the fullness thereof;
The world, and they that dwell therein.
For he hath founded it upon the seas,
And established it upon the floods.
Who shall ascend into the hill of the Lord?
Or who shall stand in his holy place?
He that hath clean hands, and a pure heart;
Who hath not lifted up his soul unto vanity,
      nor sworn deceitfully.
He shall receive the blessing from the Lord,
And righteousness from the God of his salvation.
This is the generation of them that seek him, that seek
      thy face, O Jacob.
Lift up your heads, O ye gates;
And be ye lifted up, ye everlasting doors;
And the King of glory shall come in.
Who is this King of glory?
The Lord strong and mighty, the Lord mighty in battle.
Lift up your heads, O ye gates;
Even lift them up, ye everlasting doors;
And the King of glory shall come in.
Who is this King of glory?
The Lord of hosts, he is the King of glory.

A SONG OF DAVID

A Stanza on Freedom

JAMES RUSSELL LOWELL

You cannot read these poems without a responsive thrill.   They call like trumpets to hearts of courage.

They are slaves who fear to speak
For the fallen and the weak;
They are slaves who will not choose
Hatred, scoffing, and abuse,
Rather than in silence shrink
From the truth they needs must think;
They are slaves who dare not be
In the right with two or three.

Boy, Bare Your Head

NANCY BYRD TURNER

Boy, bare your head when the flag goes by!
Girl, look your loyalty as it waves!
Those stars came out in a splendid sky
Over your forefathers' gallant graves;
Those stripes were fastened by heroes' hands;
Those colors flash to the farthest lands.
A bit of bunting, but how it gleams,
Fashioned of valor and woven of dreams.
The wind's in its folds, they are lifting high;
Oh, lift your hearts as the flag goes by!

Opportunity

EDWARD ROWLAND SILL

The poet speaks here not only for those who are heroic in battle, but for all who are brave to fight against obstacles.

This I beheld, or dreamed it in a dream: —
There spread a cloud of dust along the plain;
And underneath the cloud, or in it, raged
A furious battle, and men yelled, and swords
Shocked upon swords and shields.   A prince's banner
Wavered, then staggered backward, hemmed by foes.
A craven hung along the battle's edge,
And thought: "Had I a sword of keener steel —
That blue blade that the king's son bears, — but this
Blunt thing —!"   He snapt and flung it from his hand,
And lowering crept away and left the field.
Then came the king's son, wounded, sore bestead,
And weaponless, and saw the broken sword,
Hilt-buried in the dry and trodden sand,
And ran and snatched it, and with battle-shout
Lifted afresh he hewed his enemy down,
And saved a great cause that heroic day.

Say Not, the Struggle Naught Availeth

ARTHUR HUGH CLOUGH

How the pictures in the last two stanzas widen the horizon with hope and grandeur! Courage revives and glows golden in the sun.

Say not, the struggle naught availeth,
　The labor and the wounds are vain,
The enemy faints not, nor faileth,
　And as things have been they remain.

If hopes were dupes, fears may be liars;
　It may be, in yon smoke concealed,
Your comrades chase e'en now the fliers,
　And, but for you, possess the field.

For while the tired waves, vainly breaking,
　Seem here no painful inch to gain,
Far back, through creeks and inlets making,
　Comes silent, flooding in, the main.

And not by eastern windows only,
　When daylight comes, comes in the light;
In front the sun climbs slow, how slowly,
　But westward, look, the land is bright!

King Robert of Sicily

HENRY WADSWORTH LONGFELLOW

*Longfellow wrote many poetic narratives, but none with more pageantry of
color and dramatic action than this.*

Robert of Sicily, brother of Pope Urbane
And Valmond, Emperor of Allemaine,
Appareled in magnificent attire,
With retinue of many a knight and squire,
On St. John's eve, at vespers, proudly sat
And heard the priests chant the Magnificat.
And as he listened, o'er and o'er again
Repeated, like a burden or refrain,
He caught the words, "*Deposuit potentes
De sede, et exaltavit humiles*";
And slowly lifting up his kingly head
He to a learned clerk beside him said,
"What mean these words?"   The clerk made answer meet:
"He has put down the mighty from their seat,
And has exalted them of low degree."
Thereat King Robert muttered scornfully,
"'Tis well that such seditious words are sung
Only by priests and in the Latin tongue;
For unto priests and people be it known,
There is no power can push me from my throne!"
And leaning back, he yawned and fell asleep,
Lulled by the chant monotonous and deep.

When he awoke, it was already night;
The church was empty, and there was no light,

Save where the lamps, that glimmered few and faint,
Lighted a little space before some saint.
He started from his seat and gazed around,
But saw no living thing and heard no sound.
He groped towards the door, but it was locked;
He cried aloud, and listened, and then knocked,
And uttered awful threatenings and complaints,
And imprecations upon men and saints.
The sounds re-echoed from the roof and walls
As if dead priests were laughing in their stalls.

At length the sexton, hearing from without
The tumult of the knocking and the shout,
And thinking thieves were in the house of prayer,
Came with his lantern, asking, "Who is there?"
Half choked with rage, King Robert fiercely said,
"Open: 'tis I, the King! Art thou afraid?"
The frightened sexton, muttering, with a curse,
"This is some drunken vagabond, or worse!"
Turned the great key and flung the portal wide;
A man rushed by him at a single stride,
Haggard, half naked, without hat or cloak,
Who neither turned, nor looked at him, nor spoke,
But leaped into the blackness of the night,
And vanished like a specter from his sight.

Robert of Sicily, brother of Pope Urbane
And Valmond, Emperor of Allemaine,
Despoiled of his magnificent attire,
Bareheaded, breathless, and besprent with mire,
With sense of wrong and outrage desperate,
Strode on and thundered at the palace gate;
Rushed through the courtyard, thrusting in his rage
To right and left each seneschal and page,

And hurried up the broad and sounding stair,
His white face ghastly in the torches' glare.
From hall to hall he passed with breathless speed;
Voices and cries he heard, but did not heed,
Until at last he reached the banquet room,
Blazing with light, and breathing with perfume.

There on the dais sat another king,
Wearing his robes, his crown, his signet ring,
King Robert's self in features, form, and height,
But all transfigured with angelic light!
It was an Angel; and his presence there
With a divine effulgence filled the air,
An exaltation, piercing the disguise,
Though none the hidden Angel recognize.

A moment speechless, motionless, amazed,
The throneless monarch on the Angel gazed,
Who met his look of anger and surprise
With the divine compassion of his eyes;
Then said, "Who art thou? and why com'st thou here?"
To which King Robert answered, with a sneer,
"I am the King, and come to claim my own
From an impostor, who usurps my throne!"
And suddenly, at these audacious words,
Up sprang the angry guests, and drew their swords;
The Angel answered, with unruffled brow,
"Nay, not the King, but the King's Jester, thou
Henceforth shalt wear the bells and scalloped cape,
And for thy counsellor shalt lead an ape;
Thou shalt obey my servants when they call,
And wait upon my henchmen in the hall!"

Deaf to King Robert's threats and cries and prayers,
They thrust him from the hall and down the stairs;
A group of tittering pages ran before,
And as they opened wide the folding-door,
His heart failed, for he heard, with strange alarms,
The boisterous laughter of the men-at-arms,
And all the vaulted chamber roar and ring
With the mock plaudits of "Long live the King!"

Next morning, waking with the day's first beam,
He said within himself, "It was a dream!"
But the straw rustled as he turned his head,
There were the cape and bells beside his bed,
Around him rose the bare, discolored walls,
Close by, the steeds were champing in their stalls,
And in the corner, a revolting shape,
Shivering and chattering sat the wretched ape.
It was no dream; the world he loved so much
Had turned to dust and ashes at his touch!

Days came and went; and now returned again
To Sicily the old Saturnian reign;
Under the Angel's governance benign
The happy island danced with corn and wine,
And deep within the mountain's burning breast
Enceladus, the giant, was at rest.

Meanwhile King Robert yielded to his fate,
Sullen and silent and disconsolate.
Dressed in the motley garb that Jesters wear,
With look bewildered and a vacant stare,
Close shaven above the ears, as monks are shorn,
By courtiers mocked, by pages laughed to scorn,

His only friend the ape, his only food
What others left, — he still was unsubdued.
And when the Angel met him on his way,
And half in earnest, half in jest, would say,
Sternly, though tenderly, that he might feel
The velvet scabbard held a sword of steel,
"Art thou the King?" the passion of his woe
Burst from him in resistless overflow,
And lifting high his forehead, he would fling
The haughty answer back: "I am, I am the King!"

Almost three years were ended; when there came
Ambassadors of great repute and name
From Valmond, Emperor of Allemaine,
Unto King Robert, saying that Pope Urbane
By letter summoned them forthwith to come
On Holy Thursday to his city of Rome.
The Angel with great joy received his guests,
And gave them presents of embroidered vests,
And velvet mantles with rich ermine lined,
And rings and jewels of the rarest kind.
Then he departed with them o'er the sea
Into the lovely land of Italy,
Whose loveliness was more resplendent made
By the mere passing of that cavalcade,
With plumes, and cloaks, and housings, and the stir
Of jeweled bridle and of golden spur.

And lo! among the menials, in mock state,
Upon a piebald steed, with shambling gait,
His cloak of fox-tails flapping in the wind,
The solemn ape demurely perched behind,
King Robert rode, making huge merriment
In all the country towns through which they went.

The Pope received them with great pomp and blare
Of bannered trumpets, on Saint Peter's square,
Giving his benediction and embrace,
Fervent, and full of apostolic grace.
While with congratulations and with prayers
He entertained the Angel unawares,
Robert, the Jester, bursting through the crowd,
Into their presence rushed, and cried aloud:
"I am the King! Look, and behold in me,
Robert, your brother, King of Sicily!
This man, who wears my semblance to your eyes,
Is an impostor in a king's disguise.
Do you not know me? does no voice within
Answer my cry, and say we are akin?"
The Pope in silence, but with troubled mien,
Gazed at the Angel's countenance serene;
The Emperor, laughing, said, "It is strange sport
To keep a madman for thy Fool at court!"
And the poor, baffled Jester in disgrace
Was hustled back among the populace.

In solemn state the Holy Week went by,
And Easter Sunday gleamed upon the sky;
The presence of the Angel, with its light,
Before the sun rose, made the city bright,
And with new fervor filled the hearts of men,
Who felt that Christ indeed had risen again.
Even the Jester, on his bed of straw,
With haggard eyes the unwonted splendor saw,
He felt within a power unfelt before,
And kneeling humbly on his chamber floor,
He heard the rushing garments of the Lord
Sweep through the silent air, ascending heavenward.
[306]

And now the visit ending, and once more
Valmond returning to the Danube's shore,
Homeward the Angel journeyed, and again
The land was made resplendent with his train,
Flashing along the towns of Italy
Unto Salerno, and from thence by sea.
And when once more within Palermo's wall,
And seated on the throne of his great hall,
He heard the Angelus from convent towers,
As if the better world conversed with ours,
He beckoned to King Robert to draw nigher,
And with a gesture bade the rest retire;
And when they were alone, the Angel said,
"Art thou the King?"   Then, bowing down his head,
King Robert crossed both hands upon his breast,
And meekly answered him: "Thou knowest best!
My sins as scarlet are; let me go hence,
And in some cloister's school of penitence,
Across those stones, that pave the way to heaven,
Walk barefoot, till my guilty soul be shriven!"

The Angel smiled, and from his radiant face
A holy light illumined all the place,
And through the open window, loud and clear,
They heard the monks chant in the chapel near,
Above the stir and tumult of the street:
"He has put down the mighty from their seat,
And has exalted them of low degree!"
And through the chant a second melody
Rose like the throbbing of a single string:
"I am an Angel, and thou art the King!"

King Robert, who was standing near the throne,
Lifted his eyes, and lo! he was alone!
But all appareled as in days of old,
With ermined mantle and with cloth of gold;
And when his courtiers came, they found him there
Kneeling upon the floor, absorbed in silent prayer.

My Heart Leaps Up

WILLIAM WORDSWORTH

My heart leaps up when I behold
  A rainbow in the sky:
So was it when my life began;
So is it now I am a man;
So be it when I shall grow old,
  Or let me die!
The Child is father of the Man;
And I could wish my days to be
Bound each to each by natural piety.

XIII:
HINTS ON WRITING VERSE

There is something of the poet in us all. Like him, we enter by imagination into the life about us. We are thrilled by adventure, troubled by sorrow, and moved to wonder by beauty.

We seek to express our emotion in order that others may share it. Is there anybody alive who has not tried to describe a sunset, or to tell how frightened he was (or how bold!) when he heard the wind rustling like ghostly feet down a dark hall?

For the expression of many thoughts and emotions, the rhythmic language of poetry serves better than does the language of everyday speech. Perhaps you can recall now some experience which stirred your feeling and which you would like to shape into fitting verse. It may be a common experience, such as watching storm clouds blot out the sun or an airplane lift wings for flight. Your emotion may be deep as grief, or it may be light and gay, as when you laugh at the frolicsome balls of fur rolling about under the mother cat's impatient paw and busy, scrubbing tongue.

Whatever your subject and whatever your feelings, do not be content until you have expressed them so clearly that anyone reading your words can see just what you saw and feel just what you felt. Even the greatest writers have to work at their verse. Some poets rewrite their poems many times. They are not satisfied until they have found the exact words to convey their meaning, the most melodious arrangement, and the most vivid picturing phrases. Other poets rewrite very little, but turn the lines over and over in thought before they set pencil to paper.

[309]

Occasionally a long phrase or even whole lines may come into one's mind so beautiful that not a syllable needs to be changed. If this happens to you, you are fortunate indeed. When it does not happen, you may find that you can put yourself into the mood for writing by reading aloud a favorite poem or passage of prose. Sometimes you may enjoy imitating the work of a poet whom you like.

Since opening words are often the most difficult to choose, a start can sometimes be made by quoting a line. The quotation may be discarded later; or it may be kept (in quotation marks, of course) as a part of the poem. At other times, a suggestive title may serve as a spur to quicken the imagination. On pages 325 and 326 you will find a list of titles and lines, some of which may suggest a direction for your fancy's roving.

When you have a line which pleases you (strange as it may seem, the line which first shapes itself in imagination is not always the first line of the poem), let that determine your rhythmic pattern. Until you are skilled in rhythms, you may even find it useful to set down a metric key for your own guidance. For instance, suppose you had begun

The trees bore sprays of silver mist.

Your metric key would indicate four iambic feet: 4 ⌣ ＿.

If after you had added a second line, you decided to write in four-line stanzas, or quatrains, your stanza key would resemble this: 4 ⌣ ＿ a
⌣ ＿ b
⌣ ＿ a
⌣ ＿ b

A poet once said that all people are "poets in paren-thesis." If you have the desire to do it, and the will to persist in trying, you may step outside of the parenthesis
[310]

which fences you in, and become a poet in the open.   You will find no delight so keen as that which comes from shaping words into patterns of beauty.

When you find yourself in less serious mood, it affords no small pleasure to succeed in turning a book review into interesting rhyme for the school paper, or to recount in verse an amusing incident of classroom or of summer camp for the entertainment of your friends.   Well-wrought words can brighten a dull hour as effectively as the gay pattern of a picture brightens a drab wall.

The verses which follow were written by boys and girls. You who are learning the poet's craft will find them interesting.

Summer Afternoon

Turtles floating in the sunlight,
   Floating downward, down the stream,
Turning while the sun is shining,
   Whirling where the eddies gleam,

Eddies gleam in summer sunlight,
   A pebble rattles, clicks, and rolls,
Sand is washing in the eddies,
   Currents build up sandy shoals.

This is where my mind must wander,
   Here, and to the open sea
Where water sweeps and slides and washes,
   And shining spray flies up at me:

Rushing water, pounding waves,
   Trout in shady summer pools,
Damp sea winds, and sunlight flashing
   On the backs of bluefish schools;

Wide lagoons and sandy beaches,
   Ancient derelicts, sunk, unknown,
Over which in countless numbers
   Tides have washed and winds have blown.

TERENCE ANDERSON

Tides

The moon controls her horses
With bands of silver light;
And though they seem so very frail,
They hold with hands of might.

Her horses, they may champ their bits,
And churn the sea to foam;
They cannot break those silver reins
That bind them to their home.

The first horse has a coat of white
That shimmers in the sun;
His mane is gold with silver threads;
He's full of life and fun.

The other horse is meek and mild,
And of a color not so clear;
He shrinks away from every touch,
And quivers as with fear.

The moon controls her horses
With bands of silver light;
And though they seem so very frail,
They hold with hands of might.

JOSEPHINE WILLIAMS

Highways and Byways

Oh, you may take a highway,
A wide, straight highway,
A fine cement highway,
For yourself.

But give me a byway,
A rutted, narrow byway,
A turning, wooded byway,
For myself.

JOHN VANDERBILT

The Rabbit

I stopped for him,
He didn't for me.
I was large,
Yet small was he.
I stopped for him,
He didn't for me.

With a glare in his eyes
He looked at me.
I admired him,
He didn't me.

I was a human,
An animal he.
I stopped for him,
He didn't for me.

JOAN LEWISOHN

Ballad of the Sailor Ben

The sailor Ben had just been wed,
Swish! swash! and away he sped.
He sailed across the dark green seas
To the distant tropical East Indies.

The winds were calm and the waves were low,
Swish! swash! as away they go.
But half way over they met a gale;
So they took a reef in every sail.

With yellow jack they were stricken sore,
Swish! swash! and how they swore!
All were dead but two of the crew,
Sailor Ben and Captain Rew.

Sailor Ben received his pay,
Swish! swash! in Calcutta Bay.
Pearls and silks and costly teas
For his bride he bought in the East Indies.

After he'd spent four-score rupees,
Swish! swash! from the East Indies,
When he had crossed the sea again,
He kissed his bride, did the sailor Ben.

JACK MITCHELL

Elephant!

I was an elephant —
Big, stalky elephant —
 Living in the jungle
 With my mate and her cubs;
Having fun
In the red, hot sun;
 Walking on the paths
 That no one else has walked on;
Bathing in the dust
That a half year left;
 Soothing all my anger
 By uprooting trees and bushes;
Playing with my children,
Teaching them to fight —
 In red, hot sun,
 Of the dusty, rusty jungle.

Then came some animals,
Who walked on two legs,
 Walking on the paths that
 I owned for a century.
I trumpeted and bellowed
And they ran away like coyotes,
 Scared as the coyotes
 That sneak around the jungle.

Next day I tore
Through the trees and bushes,
 Roaring, shouting, trumpeting,
 Rushing through the jungle,

When suddenly I dropped
Some fifteen feet or over.
The ground I had been running on
Was many feet above me!
They came around
And lifted me to earth again;
They tied me while I struggled
To get back to my den.
I hit them with my trunk
And I knocked them over,
But they tied me all the tighter
So I could not move at all.

Now I am an elephant,
A broken-hearted elephant.
I live behind the bars
In a dirty, filthy zoo;
Eating only
What my master gives me —
With hardly any room to
Turn myself around in,
Hardly ever
Allowed to go outside.
How I yearn to
Get back to my mate and cubs —
The red, hot sun
Of the dusty, rusty jungle.

TOM SCHERMAN

After Reading Milne

What is the matter with Mary Jane?
She's just come in all wet from the rain,
She says she's been building a castle in Spain,
And couldn't she please go out again.

What is the matter with Mary Jane?
That mother said no was perfectly plain,
And now she must worry her poor little brain,
As to what will become of her castle in Spain.

RUTH POWELL

Triolet

I intended a handspring,
But it turned to a tail-flop —
Youth having its fling.
I intended a handspring:
I still hear the birds sing,
And see the stars pop.
I intended a handspring,
But it turned to a tail-flop.

MARGARET HOOVER

Spring

There are great gray ships
Upon the steel-gray river.
There are gray webs of cloud
Across the pearl-gray sky.
A gray screen of smoke
Hangs over the city.
The young trees quiver,
The young grasses shiver,
At the cold cutting wind
Passing by.

BARBARA CARROLL

Thought

The snowy breasted sea-gull
With whose wings
My thoughts soar upward
Into Heaven's far blue
Turns and swoops low
As if toward mundane things.
Alas! My soul's aspirings
Follow too.

MARGARET CURRIE

Cold

Wind — snow — ice — and sleet
Swirl together at my feet.
Fear — cold — night — and dread
Wind themselves around my head.
Why this fear of the wind's bleak breath?
'Tis the fear of the coldness of icy death.

MARGARET PARTON

Stormy Sea

When there are whitecaps on the ocean
And the biting wind blows cold,
And the long, chill lines of breakers
Across the sand are rolled;

When the sea is dark and angry,
When the beach is wet with spray,
And the seagull's scream can scarce be heard,
Then I'll be on my way.

Now down between the highest waves,
Now up upon their crest!
When there are whitecaps on the ocean,
Then my heart will be at rest.

JANET VAUGHN

The Story of the Alchemist

I sit among my flasks and jars,
And add mysterious potions to boiling lead;
I look intently at the stars
And never stop for wine or bread.

. . . .

I put some zinc in an iron pot,
And melted it over a fire of coal;
I added water boiling hot —
Did other things, best left untold.
All day and night I plied my trade,
But never, never found success.
The more experiments I made,
My hopefulness grew less,
Till, wearied of a wasted life,
I traveled far, to foreign lands;
And saw much peace, and still more strife,
Far from my castle and my sands.
But of that, too, I wearied fast,
And rested not till the journey was past.

. . . .

I sit among my flasks and jars,
And add mysterious potions to boiling lead;
I look intently at the stars,
And never stop for wine or bread.

EUGENE WILLIAMS

An Incident of French History

(A Rhymed Review)

The story of a fisher lad,
"The Shadow of the Sword"
Tells how he saved Mont St. Michel,
From England's hated horde.

The English thronged the sands below,
All ready for the fray,
The French stood ready on the walls,
To use their trébuchets.
Crossbowmen sent their whistling bolts
A-flying through the air,
While English cannon balls crashed through
The ramparts here and there.

It looked as if the French might lose,
When Edmond cleared the sands,
By sign of great St. Michel's sword,
From thieving English bands.

JAMES I. WHITMAN

Our Cat

Slinky and black,
Sharply curved back,
Glinting green eyes,
Blood curdling cries;
Perched on the fence,
Every limb tense:
"Scram!"   "Get out!"   "Scat!"
That's only our cat.

JANET VAUGHN

Our Dog

Rough, shaggy furze
Tangled with burrs
Covers his back.
The color is black.
He has eyes you can trust
Though he's covered with dust
And his brain's in a fog.
He's only our dog.

JANET VAUGHN

Sandy—A Small Dog

A very ungraceful dog is Sandy;
His legs are short but they come in handy.
He has no tail except for a quiver,
And whenever he's cold it begins to shiver.
His ears are long and large and bulky,
So he hides behind them whenever he's sulky.
He runs in leaps, and jumps and bounces,
And he's quite like a Tiger except for the ounces!
A very ungraceful dog is Sandy.

ALAN ANDERSON

Lower Animals

Animal No.
462

He isn't woolly, he isn't sweet,
And he lives very close to the soles of his feet.
He has great capacity for a smile —
I give you one guess, the crocodile.

Animal No.
624

The lizard is like the one mentioned above
And in many respects he's as much of a dove.
Of the crocodile he's a small edition,
Probably because of malnutrition.

Animal No.
246

The Hamadryad jumps and bites;
I often see them late at nights.
If one should get in bed with you,
I can't advise you what to do.

ALAN ANDERSON

SOME POSSIBLE SUBJECTS FOR VERSE

The Airplane Pilot
An Abandoned Ford
The Aristocratic Cat
The Voice of the Wind
The Plaint of the History Book
A Gypsy Caravan
Gypsy Fires
Adrift
Adventure
Twilight in the Fields
The Clock at Midnight
A Song for Sailors
A Transcontinental Bus
To the First Robin
The Clown
The Dreamer
A Yellow Dog
Roller Skating
Bicycling
Late Again!
To a Friend Who Has the Mumps
Smoke
Echo
Shadows
After Rain
Winter Woods
Lullaby
A Map of Paradise
The Horse Addresses the Automobile

'*Twas now the merry month of March*

The sun had brightened the river gray

They stole their way along the stair

Before his eyes a wizard stood

Without a wind the banners waved

I felt the north wind chill as death

Beside the black and secret well

The sands stretch far away

Coconut islands, parrot-haunted woods

In the April weather

In a garden cool and green

The blue waves curl and break

The bay was white with silent light

When scuds the cloud before the gale

Wrapped in silence deep and still

Under the tree at the turn of the road

He saw two eyes of flame

An ox, long fed with musty hay

Oh, list to this incredible tale

INDEX OF TITLES

INDEX OF FIRST LINES

INDEX OF AUTHORS

[337]